The Juvenile Budget Re-Opened
by John Aikin

THE

JUVENILE BUDGET RE-OPENED:

BEING

FURTHER SELECTIONS FROM THE WRITINGS

OF

DOCTOR JOHN AIKIN.

WITH COPIOUS NOTES.

"HE, BEING DEAD, YET SPEAKETH."

NEW YORK:

HARPER & BROTHERS, PUBLISHERS,
82 CLIFF STREET.
1847.

PREFACE

OUR young readers are indebted, for most of the Contents of this little Volume, to DR. JOHN AIKIN, an English gentleman, who, during a long life, devoted much of his time and talents to benefiting his fellow-beings, by inculcating sound principles of morality, and enlarging the sphere of their knowledge. He wrote much, wrote carefully, and wrote well; for all classes, and all ages; but, such was his regard for the young, and his desire for their welfare, that no kind of occupation gave him more pleasure, than that of writing for the amusement and instruction of children; and we believe his little works for little folks have exerted the widest and happiest influence, and should be the most highly cherished, of all his productions. For, at the time that he wrote, few thought it worth their while to turn their attention to the wants of the young, supposing they would gain more credit, by addressing themselves to grown people.

To the very last, he felt attached to childhood, was pleased at the sight, and delighted with the frolicksome gambols of the young. Even when on his deathbed, as his affectionate daughter tells us, " the love of children, which had always been an amiable feature in his character, remained; and the sight of his young grandchildren, sporting around

him, and courting his attention by their affectionate caresses, had often the happy effect of rousing
him from a state of melancholy languor, and carrying at least a transient emotion of pleasure to his
heart."

This Volume consists of selections from his con-
tributions to 'Evenings at Home,' his 'Letters from
a Father to his Son,' and his miscellaneous pieces.
A former Volume of the Juvenile Series of 'THE
SCHOOL LIBRARY,' for which this was also prepared, was, as its compiler tells us, selected from the
pages of the first named of these works ; and, that
it might not be mistaken for that, which also contains some pieces by Mrs. Barbauld, it was called
by the second name, which Doctor Aikin gave the
original ; that is, 'The Juvenile Budget Opened.'

Considering the attractive character of Dr. Aikin's writings for the young, and that many interesting and instructive pieces remained on hand, the
Publishers were induced to open the book, anew,
and again cull from its contents. As this Volume
was, in great part, the result of the reopening, it
was thought no more appropriate or expressive
name could be given it, than that, of '*The Juvenile
Budget Reopened.*'

Historical, biographical, and explanatory, notes
have been inserted, wherever it was supposed they
might add to the interest or value of the subject
treated of ; and, with the help of these, we believe
there is nothing in the Volume, which our young
readers cannot easily understand.

                                         T. H. W.

Boston May, 1840.

CONTENTS.

1*

JUVENILE BUDGET REOPENED

THE FARM-YARD JOURNAL.

DEAR TOM,—Since we parted, at the breaking up, I have been, for most of the time, at a pleasant farm, where I have employed myself in rambling about the country, and assisting, as well as I could, in the work going on, at home and in the fields. On wet days, and in the evenings, I have amused myself, with keeping a journal of all the great events that have happened among us ; and hoping, that, when you are tired of the bustle of your busy town, you may receive some entertainment from comparing our transactions with yours, I have copied, for your perusal, the account of the transactions of one day, from my memorandum-book.

Pray, let me know, in return, what you are doing, and believe me, your affectionate friend,
RICHARD MARKWELL

Hazel-Farm.

JOURNAL.

June 10. Last night, we had a dreadful alarm. A violent scream was heard from the hen-roost, the geese all set up a cackle, and the dogs barked. Ned, the boy who lies over the stable, jumped up and ran into the yard, when he observed a fox, galloping away, with a chicken in his mouth, and the dogs in full chase after him. They could not overtake him, and soon returned. Upon further examination, the large white cock was found, lying on the ground, all bloody, with his comb torn almost off, and his feathers all ruffled ; and the speckled hen and three chickens lay dead, beside him. The cock recovered, but appeared terribly frightened. It seems that the fox had jumped over the garden hedge, and then, crossing part of the yard, behind the straw, had crept into the hen-roost, through a broken pale. John, the carpenter, was sent for, to make all fast, and prevent the like mischief again.

Early this morning, the brindled cow had a fine calf. Both are likely to do well. The calf is to be fattened, for the butcher.

The duck eggs, that were sitten upon by the old black hen, were hatched this day, and the ducklings directly ran into the pond, to the great terror of the hen, who went round and round, clucking, with all her might, in order to call them out, but they did not regard her. An old drake took the little ones under his care, and they swam about, very merrily.

As Dolly, this morning, was milking the new cow, that was bought at the fair, she kicked, with her hind legs, and threw down the milkpail, at the same time knocking Dolly off her stool into the dirt. For this offence, the cow was sentenced to have her head fastened to the rack, and her legs tied together.

A kite was observed to hover, a long while, over the yard, with an intention of carrying off some of the young chickens ; but the hens called their broods together, under their wings, and the cocks put themselves in order of battle, so that the kite was disappointed. At length, one chicken, not minding its mother, but straggling, heedlessly, to a distance, was descried by the kite, who made a sudden swoop, and seized it in his talons. The chicken cried out, and the cocks and hens all screamed ; when Ralph, the farmer's son, who saw the attack, snatched up a loaded gun, and, just as the kite was flying off with his prey, fired, and brought him dead to the ground, along with the poor chicken, who was killed in the fall. The dead body of the kite was nailed up against the wall, by way of warning to his wicked comrades.

In the forenoon, we were alarmed with strange noises approaching us, and, looking out, we saw a number of people with fryingpans, warmingpans, tongs, and pokers, beating, ringing, and making all possible din. We soon discovered them to be our neighbors of the next farm, in pursuit of a swarm of bees, which was hovering in the air, over their heads. The bees at length alighted on the tall pear tree, in our orchard, and hung, in a bunch, from one of the boughs. A ladder was procured, and a man, ascending, with gloves on his hands, and an apron tied over his head, swept them into a hive, which was rubbed on the inside with honey and sweet herbs. But, as he was descending, some bees, which had got under his gloves, stung him, in such a manner, that he hastily threw down the hive, upon which, the greater part of the bees fell out, and began, in a rage, to fly among the crowd, and sting all upon whom they lit. Away scampered the people, the women shrieking, the children roaring ; and poor Adam, who had held the hive, was assailed so furiously, that he was obliged to throw himself on the ground, and creep under the gooseberry bushes. At length, the bees began to return to the hive, in which the queen-bee had remained ; and, after a while, all being quietly settled, a cloth was thrown over it, and the swarm was carried home.

About noon, three pigs broke into the garden, where they were eating the carrots and turnips, and doing a great deal of mischief, by trampling upon the beds, and rooting up the plants with their snouts ; when they were espied by old Towzer, the mastiff, who ran among them, and, laying hold of their long ears with his teeth, made them squeal most dismally, and get out of the garden, as fast as they could.

Roger, the ploughman, when he came for his dinner, brought word, that he had discovered a partridge's nest, with sixteen eggs, in the corn-field. Upon hearing which, the farmer went out, and broke them all ; saying, that he did not choose to rear birds upon his corn.

A sheep-washing was held, this day, at the millpool, when seven score were well washed, and then penned in the high meadow, to dry. Many of them made great resistance, at being thrown into the water; and the old ram, being dragged to the brink, by a boy at each horn, and a third pushing behind, by a sudden spring, threw two of them into the water, to the great diversion of the spectators.

Towards the dusk of the evening, the Squire's mongrel greyhound, which had been long suspected of worrying sheep, was caught in the act. He had killed two lambs, and was making a hearty meal upon one of them, when he was disturbed by the approach of the shepherd's boy, and directly leaped over the hedge, and made off. The dead bodies were taken to the Squire's, with an indictment of wilful murder against the dog. But, when they came to look for the culprit, he was not to be found, in any part of the premises, and is supposed to have fled his country, through consciousness of his heinous offence.

Joseph, who sleeps in the garret, at the old end of the house, after having been some time in bed, came down stairs, in his night-gown, as pale as ashes, and frightened the maids, who were going up. It was some time, before he could tell what was the matter; at length, he said he had heard some dreadful noises over head, which, he was sure, must be made by some ghost, or evil spirit; nay, he thought he had seen something moving, though he owned he durst hardly lift up his eyes. He concluded, with declaring, that he would rather sit up all night, in the kitchen, than go to his room, again. The maids were almost as much alarmed as he, and did not know what to do; but the master, overhearing their talk, came out, and insisted upon their accompanying him to the spot, in order to search into the affair. They all went into the garret, and, for a while, heard nothing; when the master ordered the candle to be taken away, and every one to keep quite still. Joseph and the maids kept close to each other, and trembled, every limb. At length, a kind of groaning, or snoring, began to be heard, which grew louder and louder, with intervals of a strange sort of hissing. "That's it!" whispered Joseph, drawing back towards the door; the maids were ready to sink; and even the farmer himself was a little disconcerted. The noise seemed to come from the rafters, near the thatch. But soon, a glimpse of moonlight, shining through a hole at the place, plainly discovered the shadow of something stirring; and, on looking intently, an appearance like feathers was perceived. The farmer now began to suspect what the case was; and, ordering up a short ladder, bade Joseph climb to the spot, and thrust his hand into the hole. This he did, rather unwillingly, and soon drew it back, crying, loudly, that he was bit. However, gathering courage, he put it in again, and pulled out a large white owl, another, at the same time, being heard to fly away. The cause of the alarm was now made clear enough; and poor Joseph, after being heartily jeered by the maids, though they had been as much frightened as he, sneaked into bed again, and the house soon became quiet.

THE GRASS TRIBE.

TUTOR,——GEORGE,——HARRY.

Harry. PRAY, what is that, growing on the other side of the hedge ?

George. Why, it is wheat ; do n't you see it is in ear ?

H. Yes ; but it seems too short for wheat ; and that, which we just now passed, is not in ear, by a great deal.

G. Then, I do not know what it is. Pray, sir, will you tell us ?

Tutor. I do not wonder you are puzzled about it. It is a sort of grass, sown for hay, and is called *ryegrass.*

H. But how happens it, that it is so very much like wheat ?

T. There is no great wonder in that ; for all wheat is really a kind of grass. And, on the other hand, if you were a Liliputian,* every species of grass would appear to you amazing large wheat.

G. Then, there is no difference between wheat and grass, but the size ?

T. None, at all.

* An inhabitant of Liliput, a fabled country of dwarfs.

H. But we eat wheat ; and grass is not good to eat.

T. It is only the seeds of wheat that we eat. We leave the stalks and leaves for cows and horses.   Now we might eat the seeds of grass, if they were big enough to be worth gathering ; and some particular kinds are, in fact, eaten in certain countries.

H. But are wheat and barley really grass ?

T. Yes ; they are a species of that great family of plants, which botanists call *grasses* ; and I will take this opportunity of telling you something about them.   Go, George, and pull us up a root of that ryegrass.   Harry and I will sit down on this stile, till you come to us.

H. Here is grass enough, all round us.

T. Well, then, pull up a few roots, that you see in ear.

G. Here is the grass.

H. And here is mine.

T. Well ; spread them all in a handkerchief, before us.   Now, look at the roots of them all. What do you call them ?

G. I think they are what you have told us are *fibrous* roots.

T. Right ; they consist of a bundle of strings. Then, look at their stalks,—you will find them jointed and hollow, like the straw of wheat.

H. So they are.

T. The leaves, you see, of all the kinds, are very long and narrow, tapering to a point, at their ends.   Those of wheat, you know, are the same.

H. Yes ; they are so like grass, at first, that I can never tell the difference.

T. Next, observe the ears, or heads. Some of these, you see, are thick and close, exactly like those of wheat or barley ; others are more loose and open, like oats. The first are generally called *spikes*, the second, *panicles*. If you examine them closely, you will find that they all consist of a number of distinct husky bodies, which are, properly, the flowers ; each of which is succeeded by a single seed. I dare say, you have picked ears of wheat.

H. O yes, I am very fond of them.

T. Well, you found that the grains all lay single, contained in a scaly husk, making a part of the ear, or head. Before the seed was formed, there was a flower in its place ; I do not mean a gay, fine-colored flower, but a few scales, with threads coming out among them, each crowned with a white tip. And, soon after the ears of wheat appear, you will find their flowers open, and these white tips coming out of them. This is the structure of the flowers and flowering heads of every one of the grass tribe.

G. But what are the *beards* of wheat ?

T. The beards are bristles, or points, running out from the ends of the husks. They are properly called *awns*. Most of the grass tribe have something of these, but they are much longer in some kinds than in others. In barley, you know, they are very long, and give the whole field a sort of downy or silky appearance, especially when waved by the wind.

H. Are there the same kinds of grain and grass in all countries ?

T. No. Grain is, in all countries, the product of cultivation ; and different sorts are found best to suit different climates. Thus, in the northern parts of the temperate zone, oats and rye are chiefly raised. In the middle and southern, barley and wheat. Wheat is, universally, the species preferred for bread ; but there are various kinds of it, differing from each other, in size of grain, firmness, color, and other qualities.

H. Where does the best wheat grow ?

T. Wheat is better suited to warm than to cold climates, and *it* is only by great attention, and upon particular soils, that it is made to succeed well, in the latter. On the other hand, the torrid zone is too hot for wheat, and our other grains ; and there, rice and Indian corn are chiefly cultivated.

G. I have seen heads of Indian corn as thick as my wrist. But they do not look at all like wheat.

T. Yes ; the seeds all grow single, in a sort of chaffy head ; and the stalk and leaves resemble those of the grass tribe, but of a gigantic size. But there are other plants of this family, which perhaps you have not thought of.

G. What are they ?

T. Canes and reeds ;—from the sugar-cane and bamboo of the tropics, to the common reed of our ditches, of which you make arrows. All these have the general character of the grasses.

H. I know that reeds have very fine, feathery heads, like the tops of grass.

T. They have so. And the stalks are composed of many joints ; as are also those of the sugar-cane, and the bamboo, of which fishing-rods and walking-sticks are often made. Some of these are very tall plants, but the seeds of them are small, in proportion, and not useful for food. But there is yet another kind of grass-like plants, common among us.

G. What is that ?

T. Have you not observed, in the marshes, and on the sides of ditches, a coarse, broader-leaved sort of grass, with large, dark-colored specks ? This is *sedge*, in Latin, *carex*, and there are many sorts of it.

H. What is it good for ?

T. It is eaten by cattle, both in its green and dry state ; but is inferior, in quality, to good grass.

G. What is it, that makes one kind of grass better than another ?

T. There are various properties which give value to grasses. Some spread more, than others, resist frost and drought better, yield a greater crop of leaves, and are, therefore, better for pasturage and hay. The juices of some are more nourishing and sweet, than others. In general, however, different grasses are suited to different soils ; and, by improving soils, the quality of the grass is improved.

G. Does grass grow in all countries ?

T. Yes ; the green turf, which naturally cov-

2*

ers fertile soil, in all countries, is chiefly composed of grasses, of various kinds.   They form,
therefore, the verdant carpet extended over the
earth ; and, humble as they are, they contribute
more to beauty and utility, than any other part of
the vegetable creation.

H. What ! more than trees ?

T. Yes, certainly.   A land, entirely covered
with trees, would be gloomy, unwholesome, and
scarcely inhabitable ; whereas the meadow, the
down, and the corn-field, afford the most agreeable prospects to the eye, and furnish every necessary, and many of the luxuries, of life.   Give
us corn and grass, and what shall we want for
food ?

H. Let me see, what should we have ?   There
are bread and flour, for puddings,—

G. Aye, and milk, for you know cows live on
grass and hay ; so there are cheese and butter,
and all things that are made of milk.

T. And are there not all kinds of meat, too,
and poultry ? And then for drink, there are beer
and ale, which are made from barley.   For all
of these, we are chiefly indebted to the grasses.

G. Then, I am sure, we are very much obliged
to the grasses.

T. Well, let us now walk homewards.   Some
time hence, you shall make a collection of all the
kinds of grasses, and learn to know them from
each other.

THE DISCONTENTED SQUIRREL.

IN a pleasant wood, on the western side of a ridge of mountains, there lived a Squirrel, who had passed two or three years of his life very happily. At length, he began to grow discontented, and, one day, fell into the following soliloquy :

What, must I spend all my time in this spot, running up, and down the same trees, gathering nuts and acorns, and dozing away, months together, in a hole ! I see a great many of the birds, who inhabit this wood, ramble about to a distance, wherever their fancy leads them, and, at the approach of Winter, set out for some remote country, where they enjoy Summer weather all the year round. My neighbor Cuckoo tells me he is just going ; and even little Nightingale will soon follow. To be sure, I have not wings, like them, but I have legs nimble enough ; and if one does not use them, one might as well be a mole* or a

---

* The *Mole* is a small animal, which lives under ground, and often does much mischief in the fields, by loosening the earth, raising hills, and destroying the roots of corn, grass, and other vegetables. Its sense of seeing is very feeble ; but that of hearing is very delicate and quick. The species which does so much mischief in Europe, is not found with us ; it is covered with soft, black hair, and has a pointed muzzle. In different parts of Europe, they are so numerous, and do so much injury to the farmer, that there are people there, called Mole-catchers, who make it a business to catch and destroy moles.

dormouse.* I dare say, I could easily reach to that blue ridge, which I see from the tops of the trees ; which, no doubt, must be a fine place, for the sun comes directly from it every morning, and it often appears all covered with red, and yellow, and the finest colors imaginable. There can be no harm, at least, in trying ; for I can soon get back again, if I don't like it. I am resolved to go, and I will set out to-morrow morning.

When Squirrel had taken this resolution, he could not sleep all night, for thinking of it ; and, at peep of day, prudently taking with him as much provision as he could conveniently carry, he began his journey, in high spirits. He presently reached the outside of the wood, and entered upon the open moors, that reached to the foot of the hills. These he crossed, before the sun was very high ; and then, having eaten his breakfast, with an excellent appetite, he began to ascend. It was heavy, toilsome work, scrambling up the steep sides of the mountains ; but Squirrel was used to climbing ; so, for a while, he proceeded expeditiously. Of-

* The *Dormouse* is a small animal, varying, in size, from a mouse to a rat. It has soft fur, a hairy, and even tufted tail, a lively eye, and presents a considerable degree of elegance in its appearance. It is of a tawny red, and sometimes brown, color. There are several species ; as, the Fat Dormouse, the Wood Dormouse, the Garden Dormouse, and the Common Dormouse. They feed on nuts, acorns, fruit, and other vegetables. Some of them live on trees, like squirrels ; others burrow in the ground. They pass the Winter in a torpid state. When they move about, they walk, or rather leap, on their hind legs, bounding two or three feet at a time, in which movement, they are aided by their long, stiff tail.

ten, however, was he obliged to stop, and take breath ; so that it was a good deal past noon, before he had arrived at the summit of the first cliff. Here, he sat down to eat his dinner, and, looking back, was wonderfully pleased with the fine prospect. The wood in which he lived, lay far beneath his feet ; and he viewed, with scorn, the humble habitation in which he had been born and bred.

When he looked forwards, however, he was somewhat discouraged to observe, that another eminence rose above him, full as distant as that to which he had already reached ; and he now began to feel stiff and fatigued. However, after a little rest, he set out again, though not so briskly as before. The ground was rugged, brown, and bare ; and, to his great surprise, instead of finding it warmer, as he approached nearer the sun, he felt it grow colder and colder. He had not travelled, two hours, before his strength and spirits were almost spent ; and he seriously thought of giving up the point, and returning, before night should come on. While he was thus deliberating with himself, clouds began to gather round the mountain, and to take away all view of distant objects. Presently, a storm of mingled snow and hail came down, driven by a violent wind, which pelted poor Squirrel, most pitifully, and made him quite unable to move forwards or backwards. Besides, he had completely lost his road, and did not know which way to turn towards that despised home, which it was now his only desire again to reach. The storm lasted till the approach of night ; and it was as much as he could do, benumbed and weary as he was, to crawl to the hollow of a rock, at some distance, which was the best lodging he could find for the night. His provisions were spent ; so that, hungry and shivering, he crept into the furthest corner of the cavern, and, rolling himself up, with his bushy tail over his back, he succeeded in getting a little sleep, though disturbed by the cold, and the shrill whistling of the wind among the stones.

The morning broke over the distant tops of the mountains, when Squirrel, half frozen and famished, came out of his lodging, and advanced, as well as he could, towards the brow of the hill, that he might discover which way to take. As he was slowly creeping along, a hungry hawk, soaring in the air, above, descried him, and, making a stoop, carried him off in her talons. Poor Squirrel, losing his senses with the fright, was borne away, with vast rapidity, and seemed inevitably doomed to become food for the hawk's young ones, when an eagle, who had seen the hawk seize her prey, pursued her, in order to take it from her ; and, overtaking her, gave her such a blow, as caused her to drop the Squirrel, in order to defend herself. The poor animal kept falling through the air, a long time, till, at last, he alighted in the midst of a thick tree, the leaves and tender boughs of which so broke his fall, that, though stunned and breathless, he escaped without material injury, and, after lying awhile, came to himself, again. But what was his pleasure and surprise, to find himself in the very tree which contained his nest! Ah! said he, my dear native place and peaceful home! if ever I am again tempted to leave you, may I undergo, a second time, all the miseries and dangers from which I have now so wonderfully escaped.

A DIALOGUE ON DIFFERENT STATIONS IN LIFE.

LITTLE Sally Meanwell had, one day, been to pay an afternoon's visit to Miss Harriet, the daughter of Thomas Pemberton, Esq. The evening proving rainy, she was sent home in Mr. P.'s coach; and, on her return, the following conversation passed between her and her mother.

Mrs. Meanwell. Well, my dear, I hope you have had a pleasant visit.

Sally. O yes, mamma, very pleasant; you cannot think what a great many fine things I have seen. And then, it is so charming to ride in a coach!

Mrs. M. I suppose Miss Harriet showed you all her playthings.

S. O yes, such fine large dolls, so smartly dressed, as I never saw in my life, before. Then, she has a baby-house, and all sorts of furniture in it; and a grotto, all made of shells and shining stones. And then she showed me all her fine clothes, for the next ball; she has a white slip, all full of spangles, and pink ribands ; you cannot think how beautiful it looks.

Mrs M. And what did you admire the most, of all these fine things ?

S. I do not know. I admired them all ; and I think I liked riding in the coach better than all the rest. Why do not we keep a coach, mamma ? and why have not I such fine clothes and playthings as Miss Harriet ?

Mrs. M. Because we cannot afford it, my dear. Your papa is not so rich, by a great deal, as Mr. Pemberton ; and, if we were to lay out our money upon such things, we should not be able to procure food and raiment, and other necessaries, for you all.

S. But why is not papa as rich as Mr. Pemberton ?

Mrs. M. Mr P. had a large estate left him by his father ; but your papa has little, but what he gains by his own industry.

S. But why should not papa be as rich as any body else ; I am sure, he deserves it as well.

Mrs. M. Do you not think that there are a great many people, poorer than he, that are also very deserving ?

S. Are there ?

Mrs. M. Yes, to be sure. Do n't you know what a number of poor people there are, all around us, who have very few of the comforts we enjoy ? What do you think of Plowman, the laborer ? I believe you never saw him idle, in your life.

S. No ; he is gone to work, long before I am

up, and he does not return, till almost bedtime, unless it be for his dinner.

Mrs. M. Well; how do you think his wife and children live? Should you like that we should change places with them?

S. O no! they are so dirty and ragged.

Mrs. M. They are, indeed; poor creatures! but I am afraid they suffer worse evils than that.

S. What, mamma?

Mrs. M. Why, I am afraid they often do not get as much victuals as they could eat. And then, in Winter, they must be half-starved, for want of fire and warm clothing. How do you think you could bear all this?

S. Indeed, I do not know. But I have seen Plowman's wife carry great brown loaves into the house; and I remember once eating, some brown bread and milk, and I thought it very good.

Mrs. M. I believe you would not much like it, constantly; besides, they can hardly get enough of that. But you seem to know almost as little of the poor, as the young French princess did.

S. What was that, mamma?

Mrs. M. Why, there had been one year so bad a harvest in France, that numbers of the poor were famished to death. This calamity was so much talked of, that it reached the Court, and was mentioned before the young princesses. Dear me! said one of them, how *silly* that was! Why, rather than be famished, I would eat bread and cheese. Her governess was then obliged to inform her, that the greatest part of her father's

3   VIII.

subjects scarcely ever ate any thing better than brown bread, all their lives ; and that vast numbers would now think themselves very happy, to get only half the usual pittance of that.   Such wretchedness, as this, was what the princess had not the least idea of ; and the account shocked her so much, that she was glad to sacrifice all her finery, to afford some relief to the sufferings of the poor.

S. But I hope there is nobody famished in our country.

Mrs. M. I hope not ; for we have laws, by which every person is entitled to relief from the parish, or town, if he is unable to gain a subsistence ; and, were there no laws about it, I am sure it would be our duty to part with every superfluity, rather than let a fellow-creature perish, for want of necessaries.

S. Then, do you think it was wrong, for Miss Pemberton to have all those fine things ?

Mrs. M. No, my dear, if they are suitable to her fortune, and do not consume the money which ought to be employed in more useful things, for herself and others.

S. But why might not she be contented with such things as I have ; and give the money that the rest cost, to the poor ?

Mrs. M. Because she can afford, both to be charitable to the poor, and also to indulge herself in these pleasures.   But do you recollect that the children of Mr. White, the baker, and Mr. Shape, the tailor, might, with equal propriety, ask the same questions about you ?

S. How so ?

Mrs. M. Are not you as much better dressed, and as much more plentifully supplied with play-things, than they are, as Miss Pemberton is, than you ?

S. Why, I believe I am ; for, I remember Polly White was very glad of one of my old dolls ; and Nancy Shape cried for such a sash as mine, but her mother would not let her have one.

Mrs. M. Then you see, my dear, that there are many who have fewer things to be thankful for, than *you* have ; and you may also learn, what ought to be the true measure of the exactions of children, and the indulgences of parents.

S. I do not quite understand you, mamma.

Mrs. M. Every thing ought to be suited to the station in which we live, or are likely to live, and the wants and duties of it. Your papa and I do not grudge laying out part of our money, to promote the innocent pleasure of our children ; but it would be very wrong in us, to lay out so much, on this account, as would oblige us to spare in more necessary articles, as in their education, and the common household expenses required in our way of living. Besides, it would be so far from making you happier, that it would be doing you the greatest injury.

S. How could that be, mamma ?

Mrs. M. If you were now to be dressed like Miss Pemberton, don't you think you should be greatly mortified at being worse dressed, when you came to be a young woman ?

S. I believe I should, mamma ; for then, perhaps, I might go to assemblies ; and, to be sure, I should like to be as smart, then, as at any time.

Mrs. M. Well, but it would be still more improper, for us to dress you, then, beyond our circumstances, because your necessary clothes will then cost more, you know. Besides, if we were now to hire a coach, or chair, for you to go a visiting in, should you like to leave it off, ever afterwards ? But you have no reason to expect that you will be able to have those indulgences, when you are a woman. And so it is, in every thing else. The more fine things, and the more gratifications you have, now, the more you will require, hereafter ; for custom makes things so familiar to us, that, while we enjoy them less, we want them more.

S. How is that, mamma ?

Mrs. M. Why, don't you think you have enjoyed your ride in the coach, this evening, more than Miss Harriet would have done ?

S. I suppose I have ; because, if Miss Harriet liked it so well, she would be always riding, for I know she might have the coach, whenever she pleased.

Mrs. M. But if you were both told that you were never to ride in a coach again, which would think it the greater hardship ? You could walk, you know, as you have always done, before ; but she would rather stay at home, I believe, than expose herself to the cold wind, and trudge through the wet and dirt, afoot.

S. I believe so, too ; and now, mamma, I see that all you have told me is very right.

Mrs. M. Well, my dear, let it dwell upon your mind, so as to make you cheerful and contented, in your station, which, you see, is so much happier than that of many and many other children. So, now, we will talk no more, on this subject.

THE ROOKERY.

There the hoarse-voiced, hungry Rook
Near her stick-built nest doth croak,
Waving on the topmost bough.

THESE lines Mr. Stangrove repeated, pointing up to a Rookery, as he was walking in an avenue of tall trees, with his son Francis.

Francis. Is that a Rookery, papa ?

Mr. St. It is. Do you hear what a cawing the birds make ?

F. Yes, sir ; and I see them hopping about, among the boughs. Pray, are not rooks the same with crows ?

Mr. St. They are a species of crow ; but they differ from the carrion-crow and raven, in not living upon dead flesh, but upon corn, and other seeds, and grass. They indeed pick up beetles, and other insects, and worms. See, what a number of them have lighted on yonder ploughed field, almost blacking it over.

F. What are they doing ?

3*

Mr. St. Searching for grubs and worms. You see the men in the field do not molest them, for they do a great deal of service, by destroying grubs, which, if they were suffered to grow to winged insects, would do much mischief to the trees and plants.

F. But, do they not hurt the corn ?

Mr. St. Yes ; they tear up a great deal of green corn, if they are not driven away. But, upon the whole, rooks are reckoned the farmers' friends ; and they do not choose to have them destroyed.

F. Do all rooks live in Rookeries ?

Mr. St. It is the general nature of them to associate together, and on the same or adjoining trees. But this is often in the midst of woods, or natural groves. However, they have no objection to the neighborhood of man, but readily take to a plantation of tall trees, though it be close to a house ; and this is commonly called a Rookery. They will even fix their habitations on trees, in the midst of towns ; and a Rookery has been seen in a church-yard, in one of the closest parts of London.

F. I think a Rookery is a sort of town, itself.

Mr. St. It is :——a village in the air, peopled with numerous inhabitants ; and nothing can be more amusing, than to view them all, in motion, flying to and fro, and engaged in their several oc cupations. The Spring is their busiest time. Early in the year, they begin to repair their nests, or build new ones.

F. Do they all work together, or every one for itself?

Mr. St. Each pair, after they have coupled, builds its own nest; and, instead of helping, they are very apt to steal the materials from one another. If both birds go out, at once, in search of sticks, they often find, at their return, the work all destroyed, and the materials carried off; so that one of them generally stays at home, to keep watch. However, I have met with a story, which shows that they are not without some sense of the criminality of thieving. There was in a Rookery, a lazy pair of rooks, who never went out to get sticks for themselves, but made a practice of watching when their neighbors were abroad, and helped themselves, from their nests. They had served most of the community in this manner, and, by these means, had just finished their own nest; when all the other rooks, in a rage, fell upon them, at once, pulled their nest in pieces, punished them, severely, and drove them from their society.

F. That was very right; I should like to have seen it. But why do they live together, if they do not help one another?

Mr. St. They probably receive pleasure from the company of their own kind, as men, and various other creatures do. Then, though they do not assist one another, in building, they are mutually serviceable, in many ways. If a large bird of prey hovers about a Rookery, for the purpose of carrying off any of the young ones, they all unite to drive him away. When they are feeding in a flock, several are placed, as sentinels, upon the trees all round, who give the alarm, if any danger approaches. They often go a long way from home, to feed; but, every evening, the whole flock returns, making a loud cawing, as they fly, as if to direct and call in the stragglers. The older rooks take the lead; you may distinguish them by the whiteness of their bills, occasioned by their frequent digging in the ground, by which the black feathers at the root of the bill are worn off.

F. Do rooks always keep on the same trees?

Mr. St. Yes; they are much attached to them : and, when the trees happen to be cut down, they seem greatly distressed, and keep hovering about them, as they are falling, and will scarcely desert them, when they lie on the ground.

F. Poor things. I suppose they feel as we should, if our town was burned down, or overthrown by an earthquake.

Mr. St. No doubt! The societies of animals greatly resemble those of man; and that of rooks is like those of men, in a savage state, such as the communities of the North American Indians. It is a sort of league, for mutual aid and defence, but in which every one is left to do as he pleases, without any obligation to employ himself for the whole body. Others unite, in a manner resembling more civilized societies of men. This is the case with the beavers. They perform great public works, by the united efforts of the whole community, such as damming up streams, and constructing mounds, for their habitations. As these are works of great art and labor, some of them must, probably, act under the direction of others, and be compelled to work, whether they will or not. Many curious stories are told to this purpose by those, who have observed them, in their remotest haunts, where they exercised their full sagacity.

F. But are they all true ?

Mr. St. That is more than I can answer for : yet, what we certainly know, of the economy of bees, may justify us in believing extraordinary things, of the sagacity of animals. The society of bees goes further, than that of beavers, and, in some respects, beyond most, among men themselves. They not only inhabit a common dwelling, and perform great works, in common, but they lay up a store of provision, which is the property of the whole community, and is not used, except at certain seasons, and under certain regulations. A bee-hive is a true image of a commonwealth, where no member acts for himself, alone, but for the whole body.

F. But there are drones,* among them, who do not work, at all.

* The *Drone* is a male bee. It is styled a drone, or sluggard, because it makes no honey.

A community of bees consists of three classes ; namely, *laborers* or *neuters,* (as they are called by Naturalists,) of which there are from fifteen to twenty thousand, and, sometimes, even thirty thousand ; *males* or *drones,* which number from six or eight hundred to a thousand, or more ; and a single *female,* who is at the head of the community, and is called the *queen.*

Mr. St. Yes ; and, at the approach of Winter they are driven out of the hive, and left to perish with cold and hunger. But I have not leisure, at present, to tell you more about bees. You shall, one day, see them at work, in a glass hive. In the mean time, remember one thing, which applies to all the societies of animals ; and I wish it did as well to all those of men, likewise.

F. What is that ?

Mr. St. The principle, upon which they all associate, is, to obtain some benefit for the whole body, not to give particular advantages to a few

DIALOGUE ON THINGS TO BE LEARNED.

BETWEEN MAMMA AND KITTY.

Kitty. PRAY, mamma, may I leave off working ? I am tired.

Mamma. You have done very little, my dear ; you know, you were to finish all that hem.

K. But I had rather write, now, mamma, or read, or get my French grammar.

M. I know very well what that means, Kitty ; you had rather do any thing, but what I set you about.

K. No, mamma ; but you know I can work very well, already, and I have a great many other things to learn. There is Miss Rich, that cannot sew half so well as I can, and she is learning music and drawing, already, besides dancing, and I do not know how many other things. She tells me, that they hardly work, at all, in their school.

M. Your tongue runs at a great rate, my dear ; but, in the first place, you cannot sew very well, for, if you could, you would not have been so long in doing this little piece. Then, I hope you will allow, that mammas know better, what it is proper for their little girls to learn, than they do themselves.

K. To be sure, mamma ; but, as I suppose I must learn all these things, some time or other, I thought you would like to have me begin them, soon, for I have often heard you say, that children cannot be set too early about that which is necessary for them to do.

M. That is very true. But all things are not equally necessary, to every one ; some, that are very suitable for one, are scarcely proper, at all, for others.

K. Why, mamma ?

M. Because, my dear, it is the purpose of all education, to fit persons for the station, in which they are hereafter to live ; and you know, there are very great differences, in that respect, both among men and women.

K. Are there ? I thought all *ladies* lived alike.

M. It is usual to call all well-educated women, who have no occasion to work for their livelihood, *ladies* ; but, if you will think a little, you must see that they live very differently from each other, for their fathers and husbands are in very different ranks and situations in the world, you know.

K. Yes ; I know that some are clergymen, and

some are lawyers, and some are merchants, and some are doctors, and some are shopkeepers, and some are farmers, and some are mechanics.

M. Well; and do you think the wives and daughters of all these persons can have just the same things to do, and the same duties to perform ?   You know how I spend my time ; I have to go to market and provide for the family, to look after the servants, to help in taking care of you, and the other children, and in teaching you to see that your clothes are in proper condition, and assist in making and mending for myself, and you, and your papa.   All this is my necessary duty ; and, besides this, I must go out a visiting, to keep up our acquaintance ; this I call partly business, and partly amusement.   Then, when I am tired, and have done all that I think necessary, I may amuse myself with reading, or in any other proper way.   Now, a great many of these employments do not belong to Mrs. Wealthy, or Mrs. Rich, who have housekeepers and governesses, and servants, of all kinds, to do every thing for them.   It is very proper, therefore, for them to pay more attention to music, drawing, ornamental work, and any other elegant manner of passing their time, and making themselves agreeable.

K. And shall I have all the same things to do, mamma, that you have ?

M. It is impossible, my dear, to foresee what your future station will be ; but you have no reason to expect, that, if you have a family, you will have fewer duties to perform, than I have.   This is the way of life for which your education should prepare you ; and every thing will be useful and important for you to learn, in proportion as it will qualify you for this.

K. But, when I am a young lady, shall not I have to visit, and go to places of amusement, as the Miss Wilsons and Miss Johnsons do ?

M. It is very likely you may indulge in some amusements ; but, even then, you will have several more serious employments, which will take up a much greater part of your time ; and, should you not do them properly, you will have no right to partake of the others.

K. What will they be, mamma ?

M. Why, don't you think it proper that you should assist me, in my household affairs, a little, as soon as you are able ?

K. Oh, yes, mamma ; I should be very glad to do that.

M. Well, consider what talents will be necessary, for that purpose ; will not expertness with your needle be one of the very first qualities ?

K. I believe it will.

M. Yes ; and not only in assisting me, but in making things for yourself. You know how we admired Miss Smart's ingenuity, when she was with us, in contriving and making so many articles of her dress, for which she must otherwise have gone to the milliner's, which would have cost a great deal of money.

K. Yes, she made my pretty bonnet, and she made you a very handsome cap.

4   VIII.

M. Very true ; she was so clever, as not only to furnish herself with these things, but to oblige her friends with some of her work. And I dare say, she does a great deal of plain work, also, for herself and her mother. Well, then, you are convinced of the importance of this business, I hope.

K. Yes, mamma.

M. Reading and writing are such necessary parts of education, that I need not say much to you about them.

K. O no, for I love reading, dearly.

M. I know you do, if you can get entertaining stories, to read ; but there are many things, also, to be read for instruction, which perhaps may not be so pleasant at first.

K. But what need is there of so many books of this sort ?

M. Some are to teach you your duty to your Maker, and your fellow-creatures, of which I hope you are sensible you ought not to be ignorant. Then, it is very right to be acquainted with geography ; for you remember the English story of poor Miss Blunder, who was laughed at, for saying, that if she ever went to France, it should be by land.

K. That was because England is an Island, and all surrounded with water, was it not ?

M. Yes ; Great Britain, which contains both England and Scotland, is an island. Well, it is very useful to know something of the nature of plants, and animals, and minerals, because we are always using some one or other of them. Something, too, of the heavenly bodies, is very proper to be known, both that we may admire the power and wisdom of God, in creating them, and that we may not make foolish mistakes, when their motion and properties are the subject of conversation. The knowledge of history, too, is very important, especially that of our own country ; and, in short, every thing, that makes part of the conversation of rational and well-educated people, ought, in some degree, to be studied by every one who has proper opportunities.

K. Yes ; I like some of those things very well. But pray, mamma, what do I learn French for,— am I ever to live in France ?

M. Probably not, my dear ; but there are a great many books, written in French, that are very well worth reading ; and it may, every now and then, happen, that you may be in company with foreigners, who cannot speak English, and, as they almost all talk French, you may be able to converse with them, in that language.

K. Yes ; I remember there was a gentleman, here, that came from Germany, I think, and he could hardly talk a word of English, but papa and you could talk with him, in French ; and I wished very much to be able to understand what you were saying, for I believe part of it was about me.

M. It was. Well then, you see the use of French. But I cannot say this is a necessary part of knowledge, to young women in general, only it is well worth acquiring, if a person has leisure and opportunity.   I will tell you, however, what is quite necessary for one in your station, and that is, to write a good hand, and to cast accounts well.

K. I should like to write well, because then I could send letters to my friends, when I pleased, and it would not be such a scrawl as our maid Betty writes, which, I dare say, her friends can hardly make out.

M. She had not the advantage of learning, when young, for you know she taught herself, since she came to us, which was a very sensible thing of her, and I suppose she will improve. Well, but a knowledge of accounts is almost as necessary as of writing ; for how could I cast up all the market bills, and tradesmen's accounts, and keep my house-books, without it ?

K. And what is the use of that, mamma ?

M. It is of use to prevent our being overcharged in any thing, and to know, exactly, how much we spend, and whether or not we are exceeding our income, and in what articles we ought to be more saving.   Without keeping accounts, the richest man might come to ruin, before he knew his affairs were going wrong ?

K. But do women always keep accounts ?   I thought that was, generally, the business of the men.

M. It is their business to keep the accounts belonging to their trade, or profession, or estate ; but it is the business of their wives to keep all the household accounts : and a woman in almost any rank is to blame, if she does not take upon her this necessary office. I remember a remarkable instance of the benefit which a young lady derived from an attention to this point. An eminent merchant failed, for a great sum.

K. What does that mean, mamma ?

M. That he owed a great deal more than he could pay. His creditors, that is, those to whom he was indebted, on examining his accounts, found great deficiencies, which they could not make out ; for he had kept his books very irregularly, and had omitted to put down many things, which he had bought and sold. They suspected, therefore, that great waste had been made in the family expenses ; and they were the more suspicious of this, as a daughter, who was a very genteel young lady, was his housekeeper, his wife being dead. She was told of this ; upon which, when the creditors were all met, she sent them her housebooks, for their examination. They were all written in a very fair hand, and every single article was entered, with the greatest regularity, and the sums were all cast up, with perfect exactness. The gentlemen were so highly pleased with this proof of the young lady's ability, that they all agreed to make her a handsome present out of the effects ; and one of the richest of them, who was in want of a good wife, soon after paid his addresses to her, and married her.

K. That was very fortunate, for I suppose she took care of her poor father, when she was rich.

4*

But I shall have nothing of that sort to do, for a great while.

M. No ; but young women should keep their own accounts of clothes and pocket-money, and other expenses, as I intend you shall do, when you grow up.

K. Am not I to learn dancing, and music, and drawing, too, mamma ?

M. Dancing you shall certainly learn, pretty soon, because it is not only an agreeable accomplishment, in itself, but is useful in forming the body to ease and elegance, in all its motions. As to the other two, they are ornamental accomplishments, which, though a woman of middling station may be admired for possessing, yet she will never be censured for being without. The propriety of attempting to acquire them must depend on natural genius for them, and upon leisure, and other accidental circumstances. For some, they are too expensive, and many are unable to make such progress in them, as will repay the pains of beginning. There is time enough, however, for us to think about these things ; and, at any rate, they are not to be commenced, until you have made a very good proficiency in what is useful and necessary. But I see you have now finished what I set you about, so you shall take a walk with me into the market-place, where I have two or three things to buy.

K. Shall not we call at the bookseller's, to inquire for those new books that Miss Reader was talking about ?

M. Perhaps we may. Now, lay up your work, neatly, and put on your hat and tippet.

MOUSE, LAP-DOG, AND MONKEY.

A FABLE.

A POOR little Mouse, being half-starved, ventured, one day, to steal from behind the ceiling, while the family were at dinner, and, trembling all the while, picked up a few crumbs, which were scattered on the ground. She was soon observed, however ; every body was immediately alarmed ; some called for the cat ; others took up whatever was at hand, and endeavored to crush her to pieces ; and the poor, terrified animal was driven round the room, in an agony of terror. At length, however, she was fortunate enough to gain her hole, where she sat, panting with fatigue. When the family were again seated, a Lap-dog and a Monkey came into the room. The former jumped into the lap of his mistress, fawned upon every one of the children, and made his court so effectually, that he was rewarded with some of the best morsels of the entertainment. The Monkey, on the other hand, forced himself into notice by his grimaces. He played a thousand little mischievous tricks, and was regaled, at the appearance of the dessert, with plenty of nuts and apples. The unfortunate little Mouse, who saw, from her hiding place, every thing that passed, sighed, in anguish of heart, and said to herself, " Alas ! how ignorant was I, to imagine that poverty and distress are always sufficient recommendations to the charity of the opulent. I now find, that whoever is not master of fawning and buffoonery, is but ill qualified for a dependant, and will not be suffered even to pick up the crumbs that fall from the table."

ON THE MARTIN.

Look up, my dear, (said his papa, to little William,) at those birdsnests above the chamber-windows, beneath the eaves of the house. Some, you see, are but just begun ; there being nothing but a little clay stuck against the wall. Others are half finished ; and others are quite built, close and tight, leaving nothing but a small hole, for the birds to go in and come out at.

What nests are they ? said William.

They are Martins' nests, replied his father ; and there you see the owners. How busily they fly backwards and forwards, bringing clay and dirt in their bills, and laying it upon their work, forming it into shape with their bills and feet ! The nests are built very strong and thick, like a mud wall, and are lined with feathers, to make a soft bed for the young. Martins are a kind of swallows. They feed on flies, gnats, and other insects ; and always build, in towns and villages, about the houses. People do not molest them, for they do good, rather than harm ; and it is very amusing to view their manners and actions. See, how swiftly they swim through the air, in pursuit of their prey ! In the morning, they are up by daybreak, and twitter about your window, while you are asleep in bed ; and, all day long, they are upon the wing, getting food for themselves and their young. As soon as they have caught a few flies, they hasten to their nests, pop into the hole, and feed their little ones. I will tell you a story, about the great care they take of their young. A pair of Martins once built their nest in a porch ; and, when they had young ones, it happened, that one of them, climbing up to the hole before he was fledged, fell out, and, striking upon the stones, was killed. The old birds, perceiving this accident, went and procured short bits of strong straw, and fastened them with mud, all round the hole of the nest, like palisades, in order to keep the other little ones from tumbling after their poor brother.

How cunning that was ! cried William.

Yes, said his father : and I can tell you another story of their sagacity, and also of their disposition to help one another. A saucy cock-sparrow (you know what impudent rogues they are !) took possession of a Martin's nest, whilst the owner was abroad ; and, when he returned, the sparrow put his head out of the hole, and pecked at the Martin, with open bill, as he attempted to enter his own house. The poor Martin was sadly provoked at this injustice, but was unable, by his own strength, to right himself. So he flew away, and gathered a number of his companions, who all came, with bits of clay in their bills, with which they plastered up the hole of the nest, and kept the sparrow in prison, who died miserably, for want of food and air.

He was rightly served, said William.

So he was, rejoined papa. Well; I have more to say about the sagacity of these birds. In Autumn, when it begins to be cold weather, the Martins and other swallows assemble, in great numbers, upon the roofs of high buildings, and prepare for their departure to a warmer country; for, as all the insects here die in the Winter, they would have nothing to live on, if they were to stay. They take several short flights, in flocks, round and round, in order to try their strength, and then, on some fine, calm day, they set out, together, for a long journey, southwards, over sea and land, to a very distant country.

But, how do they find the way? said William.

We say, answered his father, that they are taught by instinct; that is, God has implanted in their minds a desire of travelling, at the season which He knows to be proper, and has also given them an impulse to take the right direction. They steer their course through the wide air, directly to the proper spot. Sometimes, however, storms and contrary winds meet them, and drive the poor birds about, till they are quite spent, and fall into the sea, unless they happen to meet with a ship, on which they can light, and rest themselves. Some swallows are supposed to go as far as the middle of Africa, to spend the Winter, where the weather is always warm, and insects are to be met with, all the year. In Spring, they take another long journey, back again, to northern countries. Sometimes, when we have fine weather very early, a few of them come too soon; so that, when it changes to frost and snow, again, the poor creatures are starved, for want of food, or perish with the cold. Hence arises the proverb,

" One swallow does not make a Summer."

But, when a great many of them have come, we may be sure that Winter is over, so that we are always very glad to see them again. The Martins find their way back, over a vast length of sea and land, to the very same villages and houses, where they were bred. This has been discovered by catching some of them, and marking them. They repair their old nests, or build new ones, and then lay eggs, and hatch their young. Pretty things! I hope you will never knock down their nests, or take their eggs, or young ones; for, as they come such a long way to visit us, and lodge in and about our houses, without fear, we ought to use them kindly.

ON THE OAK.

A DIALOGUE.

TUTOR,—GEORGE,—HARRY.

Tutor. COME, my boys, let us sit down, awhile, under yon shady tree.   I do not know how your young feet feel, but mine are almost tired.

George. I am not tired, but I am very hot.

Harry. And I am hot, and very dry, too.

T. When you have cooled yourself, you may drink out of that clear brook.   In the mean time, we will read a little out of a book, I have in my pocket.

[*They go and sit down at the foot of the tree.*]

H. What an amazing large tree !   How wide its branches spread !   Pray, what tree is it ?

G. I can tell you that.   It is an Oak.   Do n't you see the acorns ?

T. Yes, it is an Oak, one of the noblest trees that grow.   It is not only grand and beautiful, to the sight, but of the greatest importance, from its uses.

H. I should like to know something about it.

T. Very well ; then, instead of reading, we will sit, and talk about Oaks.   George, you knew the Oak, by its acorns.   Should you have known it, if there had been none ?

G. I believe not.

T. Observe, then, in the first place, that its bark is very rugged. Next, see in what manner it grows. Its great arms run out, almost horizontally, from its trunk, giving the whole tree a sort of round form, and making it spread far, on every side. Its branches are also subject to be crooked, or kneed. By these marks you might guess at an Oak, even in Winter, when quite bare of leaves. But its leaves afford a surer mark of distinction, since they differ very much from those of other trees ; being neither whole and even, at the edges, nor yet cut, like the teeth of a saw, but rather deeply scolloped, and formed into several rounded divisions. Their color is a fine, deep green. Then the fruit,—

H. Fruit !

T. Yes ; all kinds of plants have what may properly be called fruit, though we are apt to give that name, only to such as are food for man. The fruit of a plant is the seed, with what contains it. This, in the Oak, is called an acorn, which is a kind of nut, partly enclosed in a cup.

G. Acorn cups are very pretty things. I have made boats of them, and set them a swimming in a basin.

T. And, if you were no bigger than a fairy, you might use them for drinking cups, as those imaginary little beings are said to do.

> Pearly drops of dew we drink,
> In acorn cups filled to the brink.

H. Are acorns good to eat ?

5   VIII.

G. No, that they are not. I have tasted of them, and did not like them, at all.

T. In the early ages of man, before he cultivated the earth, and when he lived upon such wild products as Nature afforded, we are told that acorns made a considerable part of his food; and, at this day, I believe they are eaten in some countries. But this is in warmer climates, where they probably become sweeter and better flavored, than with us. The chief use, now made of them, is to feed hogs. In those parts of England where Oak woods are common, great herds of swine are kept, which are driven into the woods, in Autumn, when the acorns fall, and provide for themselves, plentifully, for two or three months. This, however, is a small part of the value of the Oak. You will be surprised, when I tell you, that to this tree the country owes its chief glory and security.

H. How can that be!

T. I don't know whether, in your reading, you have ever met with the story, that Athens, a famous city in Greece, consulting the oracle,* how it might best defend itself against its enemies, was advised to trust to wooden walls.

H. Wooden walls! that's odd. I should think stone walls better; for wooden ones might be set on fire.

* Among Pagans, the answer of some one reputed to be a god, to an inquiry made respecting some affair of importance. The name was also applied to the place where the answer was given, and to the god who was supposed to give it

T. True ; but the meaning was, that, as Athens was a place of great trade, and its people were skilled in maritime affairs, they ought to trust to their ships. Well, this is the case with Great Britain. As it is an island, it has no need of walls and fortifications, while it possesses ships to keep all enemies at a distance. Now, that nation has the greatest navy in the world, by which she both defends herself, and attacks other nations, when they insult her ; and this is all built of Oak.

G. Would no other wood do to build ships ?

T. None nearly so well, especially for men-of-war ; for it is the stoutest and strongest wood we have ; and therefore best fitted, both to keep sound, under water, and to bear the blows and shocks of waves, and the terrible strokes of cannon-balls. It is a peculiar excellence for this last purpose, that Oak is not so liable to splinter or shiver, as other woods, so that a ball can pass through it, without making a large hole. Did you never hear the old song,

Hearts of oak are our ships, hearts of oak are our men, &c. ?

G. No.

T. It was made at a time when England was more successful in war, than had ever before been known, and her success was properly attributed, chiefly, to her fleet, the great support of which is the British Oak.

H. This shall always be my favorite tree.

T. Had not Pope* reason, when he said, in his ' Windsor Forest,'

   " Let India boast her plants, nor envy we
     The weeping amber, or the balmy tree,
     While by our *oaks* the precious loads are borne,
     And realms commanded which those trees adorn ?"

These lines refer to its use, as well for merchant ships, as for men-of-war ; and, in fact, all our ships are built of Oak.

G. Are the masts of ships made of Oak ?

T. No ; it would be too heavy ; besides, it would not be easy to find trunks of Oak, long and straight enough for that purpose. They are made of various kinds of fir or pine, which grow very tall and taper.

G. Is Oak wood used for any thing, besides ship-building ?

T. O yes ! It is one of the principal woods for the carpenter, being employed wherever great strength and durability are required. It is used for door and window frames, and the beams that are laid in walls to strengthen them. Floors and staircases are sometimes made with it ; and, in old houses in the country, which were built when Oak was more plentiful than at present, almost all

* *Alexander Pope*, a celebrated English poet, was born in London, May 22, 1688. Soon after his birth, his father removed to Binfield, near Windsor Forest. Here, in the year 1713, he produced his poem, entitled, ' Windsor Forest.' His poetical works fill several large volumes, and some of them, as, for example, his ' Essay on Man,' have been extensively read, and much admired. He died, May 30, 1744, at the age of fifty-six, and was buried at Twickenham, where Bishop Warburton erected a monument to his memory.

the timber about them is Oak. It is, also, occasionally used for furniture, as tables, chairs, drawers, and bedsteads ; though mahogany has now much taken its place, for the better sort of articles, and the lighter and softer woods, for the cheaper ; for the hardness of Oak renders it difficult and expensive to work. It is still, however, the chief material used in mill-work, in bridge and water works, for wagon and cart bodies, for large casks and tubs, and, in England and some other countries, for the last piece of furniture for which a man has occasion. What is that, do you think, George ?

G. I do not know.

H. A coffin.

T. So it is.

H. But why should that be made of such strong wood ?

T. There can be no other reason, than that weak attachment we are apt to have for our bodies, when we have done with them, which has made men, in various countries, desirous of keeping them as long as possible, from decay. But I have not yet done with the uses of the Oak. Were either of you ever in a tanner's yard ?

G. We often go by one, at the end of the town ; but we durst not go in, for fear of the great dog.

T. But he is always chained, in the day-time.

H. Yes, but he barks so loud, and looks so fierce, that we were afraid he would break his chain.

T. I suspect you are a couple of cowards. However, I suppose you came near enough, to observe great stacks of bark in the yard.

G. O yes, there are are several.

T. Those are Oak bark, and it is used in tanning the hides.

H. What does it do to them ?

T. I will tell you. Every part of the Oak abounds in a quality called astringency, or a binding power. The effect of this is, to make the hides more close and compact, or to shrivel them up, and thereby make them firmer, and less liable to decay. The hide, when taken from the animal, after being steeped in lime and water, to get off the hair and grease, is put in a liquor made by soaking Oak bark in water. This liquor is strongly astringent, and, by stiffening the soft hide, turns it into what we call leather. Other things are also tanned for the purpose of preserving them, as fishing nets, and boat sails. This use of the bark of the Oak makes it a very valuable commodity ; and you may see people in the woods, carefully stripping the Oaks, when cut down, and piling up the bark in heaps.

G. I have seen such heaps of bark, but I thought they were only to burn,

T. No ; they are much too valuable for that. Well, but I have another use of the Oak to mention, and that is in dyeing.

H. Dyeing ! I wonder what color it can dye ?

T. Oak sawdust is a principal ingredient in dyeing fustians. By various mixtures and management, it is made to give them all the different shades of drab and brown. Then, all the parts of the Oak, like all other astringent vegetables, produce a dark blue, or black, by the addition of any preparation of iron. The bark is sometimes used, in this way, for dyeing black. And did you ever see what boys call an Oak apple ?

G. Yes, sir, I have gathered them, myself.

T. Do you know what they are ?

G. I thought they were the fruit of the Oak.

T. No ; I have told you that the acorns are the fruit. These are excrescences formed by an insect.

G. An insect ! How can an insect make such a thing ?

T. It is a sort of fly, that has a power of piercing the outer skin of the Oak boughs, under which it lays its eggs. The part then swells into a kind of ball, and the young insects, when hatched, eat their way out. Well ; this ball, or apple, is a pretty strong astringent, and is sometimes used, in dyeing black. But, in some warm countries, there is a species of Oak, which bears round excrescences of the same kind, called galls, which become hard, and are the strongest astringents known. They are the principal ingredients in the black dyes ; and common ink is made with them, and a substance called green vitriol, or copperas, which contains iron.

I have now told you the chief uses, that I can recollect, of the Oak ; and these are so important, that whoever drops an acorn into the ground, and takes proper care of it when it comes up, may be said to be a benefactor to his country. Besides, no sight can be more beautiful and majestic than a fine Oak wood. It is an ornament fit for the habitation of the best man in the land.

H. I wonder, then, that all rich gentlemen, who have ground enough, do not cover it with Oaks.

T. Many, in Europe, especially of late years, have made great plantations of these trees. But all soils do not suit them ; and then, there is another circumstance, which prevents many from being at this trouble and expense, which is, the long time an Oak takes, in growing, so that no person can reasonably expect to profit by those of his own planting. An Oak, of fifty years, is greatly short of its full growth ; and it scarcely arrives at perfection, under a century. However, it is our duty to think of posterity, as well as of ourselves ; and they, who receive Oaks from their ancestors, ought, certainly, to furnish others to their successors.

H. Then, I think, that every one, who cuts down an Oak, should be obliged to plant another.

T. Very true ; but he should plant two or three for one, for fear of accidents which may happen to them whilst they are growing. I will now repeat to you some verses describing the Oak, in its state of full growth, or, rather, of beginning decay, with the various animals living upon it ; and then we will walk.

THE OAK.

See, where yon Oak its awful structure rears,
The massy growth of twice a hundred years ;
Survey his rugged trunk, with moss o'ergrown,
His lusty arms, in rude disorder thrown,
His forking branches wide at distance spread,
And, dark'ning half the sky, his lofty head ;
A mighty castle, built by Nature's hands,
Peopled by various living tribes, he stands.
His airy top the clamorous rooks invest,
And crowd the waving boughs with many a nest.
Midway, the nimble squirrel builds his bower,
And sharp-billed pies the insect-tribes devour,
That gnaw beneath the bark their secret ways,
While, unperceived, the stately pile decays.

THE SHIP.

CHARLES OSBORN, when at home, in the holy-
days, had a visit from a schoolfellow, who was
just entered as a midshipman* on board of a man-
of-war.†   His name was Tom Hardy.   He was
a freehearted, spirited lad, and a favorite among

* A naval cadet, or young officer, whose duty it is to attend to the execution of the orders issued by the superior
officers, and assist in the necessary business of the vessel,
either aboard, or ashore.   It is the station in which a young
volunteer is trained in the several exercises necessary to acquire a sufficient knowledge of the machinery, discipline,
movements, and military operations, of a ship, in order to
qualify him for a sea-officer.

† A ship, intended for service in time of war, and also employed for the protection of persons and property, is so styled.
in seamen's language.

his companions ; but he never liked his book, and had left school, ignorant of almost every thing, he went there to learn.   What was worse, he had a contempt for learning, of all kinds, and was fond of shewing it.   " What does your father mean," says he, to Charles, " to keep you moping and studying over things of no use in the world, but to plague folks ?   Why can 't you go into the naval service, like me, and be made a gentleman of ? You are old enough, and I know you are a lad of spirit."   This kind of talk made some impression upon young Osborn.   He became less attentive to the lessons, his father set him, and less willing to enter into instructive conversation. This change gave his father much concern ; but, as he knew the cause, he thought it best, instead of employing direct authority, to attempt to give a new impression to his son's mind, which might counteract the effects of his companion's suggestions.

Being acquainted with an East-India captain, who was on the point of sailing, he went, with his son, to pay him a farewell visit on board his ship. They were shown all about the vessel, and viewed all the preparations for so long a voyage. They saw her weigh anchor* and unfurl her sails ; and they took leave of their friend, amid the shouts of the seamen, and all the bustle of departure.

Charles was highly delighted with this scene ;

* *To weigh anchor* is to raise the anchor from the ground, preparatory to a vessel's sailing.

and, as they were returning, could think and talk of nothing else. It was easy, therefore, for his father to lead him into the following train of discourse.

After Charles had been warmly expressing his admiration of the grand sight of a large ship, completely fitted out, and getting under sail, I do not wonder, (said his father,) that you are so much struck with it ; it is, in reality, one of the finest spectacles created by human skill, and one of the noblest triumphs of art, over untaught Nature. Near two thousand years ago, when Julius Cæsar* went over to England, he found the natives in possession of no other kind of vessel, than a sort of canoe, formed of wicker work, covered with hides, and no bigger than a man or two could carry. But the largest ship in Cæsar's fleet was not more superior to these, than the Indiaman,† you have been seeing, is, to what that was. The natives ventured only to paddle along the rivers and coasts, or cross small arms of the sea, in calm weather ; and Cæsar himself would have been alarmed, to be a few days out of sight of land. But the ship, we have just left, is going, by itself, to the opposite side of the globe, prepared to encounter the tempestuous winds and moun-

* *Caius Julius Cæsar*, the first Emperor of Rome, is said to have fought five hundred battles, subdued three hundred nations, taken eight hundred cities, and conquered *three millions* of men. What a great amount of sorrow and distress must he have occasioned to his fellow-beings !

† A ship, intended for the East India trade.

tainous waves of the vast southern ocean, and to find its way to its destined port, though many weeks must pass, with nothing in view but sea and sky. Now, what do you think can be the cause of this prodigious difference in the powers of man, at one period, and another?

Charles was silent.

Is it not, (said his father,) that there is a great deal more knowledge in one, than in the other?

To be sure it is, said Charles.

Father. Would it not, think you, be as impossible for any number of men, untaught, by their utmost efforts, to build and navigate such a ship, as we have seen, as to fly through the air?

Charles. I suppose it would.

F. That we may be the more sensible of this, let us consider how many arts and professions are necessary, for this purpose. Come, you shall begin to name them, and, if you forget any, I will put you in mind of them. What is the first?

C. The ship-carpenter, I think.

F. True; what does he do?

C. He builds the ship.

F. How is that done?

C. By fastening the planks and beams together.

F. But, do you suppose he can do this, as a common carpenter makes a box, or a set of shelves?

C. I do not know.

F. Do you not think that such a vast bulk requires a great deal of contrivance, to bring it into shape, and fit it for all its purposes?

C. Yes.

F. Some ships, you have heard, sail quicker than others ; some bear storms better ; some carry more lading ; some draw less water ;* and so on. You do not suppose all these things are left to chance ?

C. No.

F. In order, with certainty, to produce these effects, it is necessary to study proportions, very exactly, and to lay down an accurate scale, by mathematical lines and figures, after which to build the ship. Much has been written upon this subject, and nice calculations have been made of the resistance a ship meets with, in making her way through the water, and the best means of overcoming it ; also, of the action of the wind on the sails ; and their action in pushing on the ship, by means of the masts. All these must be understood by a perfect master of ship-building.

C. But I think I know ship-builders, who have never had an education to fit them for understanding these things.

F. Very likely ; but they have followed, by rote, the rules laid down by others ; and, as they work merely by imitation, they cannot alter and improve, as occasion may require. Then, though

* The depth of a body of water necessary to float a ship, is called its draught ; hence, a ship is said to draw so many feet of water, when she is borne up by a column of water of that particular depth, and that this draught may be more readily known, it is marked in feet on the stem and stern-post, or anterior and posterior parts of the ship, from the keel, or bottom, upwards.

common merchant ships are trusted to such buil-
ders, yet, in constructing men-of-war and India-
men, persons of science are always employed.

C. But need a captain of a ship know all
these things ?

F. It may not be absolutely necessary ; yet
occasions may frequently arise, in which it would
be of great advantage for him to be able to judge,
and give directions, in these matters. But, suppose the ship built ; what is to be done, next ?

C. I think she must be rigged.

F. Well ; who are employed for this purpose ?

C. Mast-makers, rope-makers, sail-makers,
and I know not how many other people.

F. These are all mechanical trades ; and,
though in carrying them on, much ingenuity has
been applied, in the invention of machines and
tools, yet we will not stop to consider them.
Suppose her, then, rigged ; what next ?

C. She must take in her guns and powder.

F. Stop there, and reflect, how many arts you
have now set to work. Gunpowder is one of the
greatest inventions of modern times, and has given
much superiority to civilized, over barbarous, nations. A frigate, surrounded by the canoes of all
the savages in the world, would easily beat them
off, by means of her guns ; and, were Cæsar now
alive, and to go again to England, with his fleet, a
battery of cannon would sink all his ships, and
set his legions a swimming in the sea. But the
making of gunpowder, and the casting of cannon,
are arts that require an exact knowledge of the
science of *chemistry.*

C. What is that ?

F. It comprehends the knowledge of all the properties of metals and minerals, salts, sulphur, oils, and gums ; and of the action of fire, and water, and air, upon all substances, and the effects of mixing different things together. Gunpowder is a mixture of three things, only ; saltpetre or nitre, sulphur or brimstone, and charcoal. But who could have thought such a wonderful effect would have been produced by it ?

C. Was it not first discovered by accident ?

F. Yes ; but it was by one who was making chemical experiments, and many more experiments have been employed, to bring it to perfection.

C. But need a captain know how to make gunpowder and cannon ?

F. It is not necessary, though it may often be useful to him. However, it is quite necessary that he should know how to employ them. Now, the sciences of gunnery and fortification depend entirely upon mathematical principles ; for, by these, are calculated the direction of a ball through the air, the distance to which it will reach, and the force with which it will strike any thing. All engineers, therefore, must be good mathematicians.

C. But I think I have heard of gunners, who were little better than the common men.

F. True, there is a way of doing that business, as well as many others, by mere practice ; and an uneducated man may acquire skill, in pointing a cannon, as well as in shooting with a common gun. But this is only in ordinary cases, and an abler head is required, to direct. Well, now, suppose your ship completely fitted out for sea, and the wind blowing fair; how will you navigate her?

C. I would spread the sails, and steer by the rudder.

F. Very well; but how would you find your way to the port, for which you were bound?

C. That, I cannot tell.

F. Nor perhaps can I make you exactly comprehend it; but I can show you enough to convince you, that it is an affair that requires much knowledge and early study. In former times, when a vessel left the sight of land, it was steered by observation of the sun, by day, and the moon and stars, by night. The sun, you know, rises in the east, and sets in the west; and, at noon, in these parts of the world, it is exactly south of us. These points, therefore, may be found out, when the sun shines. The moon and stars vary; however, their place, in the sky, may be known by exact observation. Then, there is one star, that always points to the north pole, and is therefore called the pole-star. This was of great use, in navigation, and the word pole-star is often used by the poets, to signify a sure guide. Do you recollect the description in Homer's ' Odyssey,'* when

* A celebrated Greek poem, in which is described the return of the Grecian prince, Ulysses, and the misfortunes which befel him, during the voyages, after the Trojan war; a war, undertaken by all Greece, to recover Helen, wife of the Spar-

Ulysses sails away by himself, from the island of Calypso, how he steers by the stars ?

C. I think I remember the lines, in Pope's translation.

F. Repeat them, then.

> *C.* " Placed at the helm, he sat, and marked the skies,
> Nor closed, in sleep, his ever-watchful eyes.
> There viewed the Pleiads,* and the Northern Team,
> And great Orion's more refulgent beam,
> To which, around the axle of the sky,
> The Bear, revolving, points his golden eye :
> Who shines, exalted, on th' etherial plain,
> Nor bathes his blazing forehead in the main."

F. Very well ; they are fine lines, indeed ! You see, then, how long ago, sailors thought it necessary to study astronomy. But, as it frequently happens, especially in stormy weather, that the stars are not to be seen, this method was subject to great uncertainty, which rendered it dangerous to undertake distant voyages. At length, near five hundred years since, a property was

tan King Menelaus, who had been forcibly carried away by Paris, the son of the king of Troy. But little is satisfactorily known of the author of the 'Odyssey,' Homer. The time of his birth and death is uncertain, and his birthplace is no less so ; seven cities claiming it to be within their borders. He is conjectured to have flourished, somewhere from the eighth to the tenth century, before Christ.

* *Pleiads,* or *Pleiades ;* the name of a cluster of seven stars. *Orion* is a constellation in the southern hemisphere, containing seventy-eight stars. *Bear ;* the name of two constellations, in the northern hemisphere, called the Great and Little Bear. The pole-star, which serves as the mariner's guide, at sea, is situated in the latter. The *Northern Team* is a cluster of seven stars, in the Great Bear.

6*

discovered in a mineral, called the magnet, or loadstone, which removed the difficulty. This was its *polarity*, or quality of always pointing to the poles of the earth, that is, due north and south. This it can communicate to any piece of iron, so that a needle, well rubbed, in a particular manner, by a loadstone, and then balanced upon its centre, so as to turn round freely, will always point to the north. With an instrument, called a mariner's compass, made of one of these needles, and a card, marked with all the points, north, south, east, and west, and the divisions between these, a ship may be steered to any part of the globe.

C. It is a very easy matter, then.

F. Not quite so easy, neither. In a long voyage, cross or contrary winds blow a ship out of her direct course, so that, without nice calculations, both of the straight track she has gone, and all the deviations from it, the sailors would not know where they were, nor to what point to steer. It is also frequently necessary, to take observations, as they call it ; that is, to observe, with an instrument, where the sun's place in the sky is, at noon, by which they can determine the *latitude*, they are in. Other observations are necessary, to determine their *longitude*. What these mean, I can show you upon the globe. It is enough now to say, that, by means of both, together, they can tell the exact spot they are on, at any time ; and then, by consulting their map, and setting their compass, they can steer right to the place they want. But all this requires a very exact knowledge of astronomy, the use of the globes, mathematics, and arithmetic, which you may suppose is not to be acquired, without much study. A great number of curious instruments have been invented, to assist in these operations; so that there is scarcely any matter, in which so much art and science have been employed, as in navigation; and none, but a very learned and civilized nation, can excel in it.

C. But how is Tom Hardy to do? for I am pretty sure, he does not understand any of these things.

F. He must learn them, if he means to come to any thing in his profession. He may, indeed, head a pressgang, or command a boat's crew, without them; but he will never be qualified to take charge of a man-of-war, or even a merchant ship.

C. However, he need not learn Latin and Greek.

F. I cannot say, indeed, that a sailor has occasion for those languages; but a knowledge of Latin makes it much easier to acquire all modern languages; and I hope you do not think them unnecessary to him.

C. I did not know they were of much importance.

F. No! Do you think that one, who may probably visit more countries in Europe, and their foreign settlements, should be able to converse in no other language than his own? If the knowledge of languages is not useful to *him*, I know not to whom it is.   He can hardly do at all, without knowing some ; and the more he understands, the better will it be for him.

C. Poor Tom ! then I fear he has not made so good a choice, as he thinks he has.

F. I fear such is the case.

Here ended the conversation.   They, soon afterwards, reached home, and Charles did not forget, to desire his father to show him, on the globe, what longitude and latitude meant.

THE TRANSMIGRATIONS* OF INDUR.

AT the time when those fabulous beings, called

Transmigration.   The passing of the soul of a person, after death, into the body of some animal.   Many of the ancients fully believed in this notion, and it is still credited by the idolatrous nations of India and China, who forbear eating any thing that has life ; will not burn wood, for fear some small insect should be in it, and thus be unintentionally destroyed ; and will redeem from strangers, any animals that they are about to kill.   Many of them will, indeed, refuse to defend themselves against the attacks of wild beasts.   The opinion of the believers in this doctrine is, that the description of animal into which the soul passes, depends upon the kind of life which the individual led.   If it had been a wicked and cruel one, the soul was supposed to enter, or, more properly, to be imprisoned in, a miserable, grovelling beast, from which, after suitable punishment, for wrong conduct, it was released, and permitted to enter the body of another human being.   If a virtuous life had been led, the soul entered some harmless, happy brute.   No Christian nation countenances this strange doctrine.

fairies and genii, were imagined to possess great powers, there lived, in the country of the Brachmans,* a man named Indur, who was distinguished, not only for that gentleness of disposition and humanity towards all living creatures, which are so much cultivated among those people, but for an insatiable curiosity respecting the nature and way of life of all animals.   In pursuit of knowledge of this kind, he would frequently spend the night among lonely rocks, or in the midst of thick forests ; and there, under shelter of a hanging cliff, or mounted upon a high tree, he would watch the motions and actions of all the animals that seek their prey in the night ; and remaining in the same spot, till the break of day, he would observe this tribe of creatures retiring to their dens, and all others coming forth, to enjoy the beams of the rising sun.   On these occasions, if he saw any opportunity of exercising his benevolence towards animals in distress, he never failed to make use of it ; and many times rescued the small birds from the pitiless hawk, and the lamb or kid from the gripe of the wolf.   One day, as he was sitting on a tree, in the forest, a little frolicsome monkey, in taking a leap from one bough to another, chanced to miss his hold, and fell, from a great height, to the ground.   As he lay there, unable to move, Indur espied a large, venomous serpent advancing, to make the poor, defenceless creature his prey.   He immediately de-

---

* *Brachman*, a philosopher, or priest of India, sometimes written Bramin, or Brahmin.

scended from his post, and, taking the little mon
key in his arms, ran with it to the tree, and gen
tly placed it upon a bough.   In the mean time,
the enraged serpent, pursuing him, overtook him,
before he could mount the tree, and bit him in the
leg.   Presently, the limb began to swell, and the
effects of the venom became visible over Indur's
whole frame.   He grew faint, sick, and pale ;
and, sinking on the ground, was sensible that his
last moments were fast approaching.   As thus he
lay, he was surprised to hear a human voice from
the tree ; and, looking up, he beheld, on the
bough where he had placed the monkey, a beautiful woman, who thus addressed him : " Indur,
I am truly grieved that thy kindness to me should
have been the cause of thy destruction.   Know,
that, in the form of the poor monkey, it was the
potent fairy, Perezinda, to whom thou gavest
succor.   Obliged to pass a certain number of
days, every year, under the shape of an animal,
I had chosen this form ; and, though not mortal,
I should have suffered extreme agonies from the
bite of the serpent, hadst thou not so humanely
assisted me.   It is not in my power to prevent
the fatal effect of the poison ; but I am able to
grant thee any wish thou shalt form, respecting
the future state of existence, to which thou art
now hastening.   Speak, then, before it be too
late, and let me show my gratitude."   " Great
Perezinda !" replied Indur, " since you design
so bounteously to return my service, this is
the request that I make.   In all my transmigra-

tions, may I retain a rational soul, with the memory of the adventures I have gone through ; and, when death sets me free from one body, may I instantly animate another, in the prime of its powers and faculties, without passing through the helpless state of infancy."—"It is granted," answered the fairy ; and, immediately breaking a small branch from the tree, and breathing on it, she threw it down to Indur, and bade him hold it fast in his hand. He did so, and presently expired.

Instantly, he found himself in a green valley, by the side of a clear stream, grazing amid a herd of Antelopes. He admired his elegant shape, sleek, spotted skin, and polished spiral horns ; and drank, with delight, of the cool rivulet, cropped the juicy herb, and sported with his companions. Soon, an alarm was given, of the approach of an enemy ; and they all set off, with the swiftness of the wind, to the neighboring immense plains, where they were soon out of the reach of injury. Indur was highly delighted with the ease and rapidity of his motions ; and, snuffing the keen air of the desert, bounded away, scarcely deigning to touch the ground with his feet. This way of life went on, very pleasantly, for some time, till, at length, the herd was one morning alarmed with noises, of trumpets, drums, and loud shouts, on every side. They started and ran, first to the right, then to the left, but were continually driven back by the surrounding crowd, which now appeared to be a whole army of hunters, with the king of the country and all his nobles, assembled, on a solemn chase, after the manner of the eastern people. And now the circle began to close, and numbers of affrighted animals, of various kinds, thronged together, in the centre, keeping as far as possible from the dangers that approached them from all quarters. The huntsmen soon came near enough to reach their game with their arrows ; and the prince and his lords shot at them, as they passed and repassed, killing and wounding great numbers. Indur and his surviving companions, seeing no other means of escape, resolved to make a bold push towards that part of the ring which was the most weakly guarded ; and, though many perished in the attempt, yet a few, leaping over the heads of the people, succeeded in getting away ; and Indur was among the number. But, whilst he was scouring over the plain, rejoicing in his good fortune and conduct, an enemy, swifter than himself, overtook him. This was a falcon, who, let loose by one of the huntsmen, dashed, like lightning, after the fugitives ; and, alighting upon the head of Indur, began to tear his eyes, with his beak, and flap his wings over his face. Indur, terrified and blinded, knew not which way he went ; and, instead of proceeding straight forwards, turned round, and came again towards the hunters. One of these, riding full speed, with a javelin in his hand, came up to him, and ran the weapon in his side. He fell down, and, with repeated wounds, was soon despatched.

When the struggle of death was over, Indur

was equally surprised and pleased, on finding himself soaring high in the air, as one of a flight of *wild geese*, in their annual migration to breed in the arctic regions. With vast delight, he sprung forward, on easy wing, through the immense fields of air, and surveyed, beneath him, extensive tracts of earth, perpetually varying, with plains, mountains, rivers, lakes, and woods. At the approach of night, the flock lighted on the ground, and fed on the green corn or grass ; and, at daybreak, they were again on wing, arranged in a regular wedge-like form, with an experienced leader at their head. Thus, for many days, they continued their journey, passing over countries inhabited by various nations, till, at length, they arrived in the remotest part of Lapland, and settled in a wide, marshy lake, filled with numerous reedy islands, and surrounded, on all sides, with dark forests of pine and birch. Here, in perfect security from man and hurtful animals, they followed the great business of breeding and providing for their young, living plentifully upon the insects and aquatic reptiles, that abounded in this sheltered spot. Indur, with great pleasure, exercised his various powers, of swimming, diving, and flying ; sailing round the islands, penetrating into every creek and bay, and visiting the deepest recesses of the woods. He surveyed, with astonishment, the sun, instead of rising and setting, making a complete circle in the heavens, and cheering the earth with a perpetual day. Here, he met with innumerable tribes of kindred birds,

7   VIII.

varying in size, plumage, and voice, but all passing their time in a similar manner, and furnished
with the same powers for providing food, and a
safe retreat for themselves and their young.   The
whole lake was covered with parties, fishing or
sporting, and resounded with their loud cries ;
while the islands were filled with their nests, and
new broods of young were continually coming
forth, and launching upon the surface of the waters.   One day, Indur's curiosity having led him
at a distance from his companions, to the woody
border of the lake, he was near paying dear for
his heedlessness ; for a fox, that lay in wait
among the bushes, sprung upon him, and it was
with the utmost difficulty that, by a strong exertion, he broke from his hold, though not without the loss of some feathers.

Summer now drawing to an end, the vast con-
gregation of water-fowl began to break up ; and
large bodies of them daily took their way southwards, to pass the Winter in climates where the
waters are never so frozen, as to become uninhab-
itable by the feathered race.   The wild geese,
to whom Indur belonged, proceeded, with their
young ones, by long, daily journies, across Sweden, the Baltic sea, Poland, and Turkey, to Les-
ser Asia, and finished their journey at the celebrated plains on the banks of the Cayster,* a noted
resort for their species, ever since the age of Ho-

* A river of Asia, the banks and neighborhood of which
were said to be much frequented by swans, and other birds.

mer,* who, in some very beautiful verses, has
described the manners and actions of the various
tribes of aquatic birds, in that favorite spot.†
Here, they soon recruited from the fatigue of their
march, and enjoyed themselves in the delicious
climate, till Winter. This season, though here
extremely mild, making the means of sustenance
somewhat scarce, they were obliged to go on excursions for food, to the cultivated lands in the
neighborhood. Having committed great depredations upon a fine field of young wheat, the owner spread a net on the ground, in which Indur,
with several of his companions, had the misfortune to be caught. No mercy was shown them;
but, as they were taken out, one by one, their
necks were all broken.

Indur was not immediately sensible of the next
change he underwent, which was into a *dormouse*,‡
fast asleep in his hole, at the foot of a bush. As
it was in a country, where the Winters are pretty
severe, he did not awake, for some weeks ; when,
a thaw having taken place, and the sun beginning
to warm the earth, he unrolled himself, one day,
stretched, opened his eyes, and, not being able to

* See note on page 64.

† " Not less their number than th' embodied cranes,
    Or milk-white swans on Asia's watery plains,
    That, o'er the windings of Cayster's springs
    Stretch their long necks, and clap their rustling wings;
    Now tower aloft, and course in airy rounds ;
    Now light with noise ; with noise the field resounds."
                                        Pope's Homer.

‡ See note on page 20.

make out where he was, he roused a female companion, whom he found by his side. When she was sufficiently awakened, and they both began to feel hungry, she led the way to a magazine of nuts and acorns, where they made a comfortable meal, and soon fell asleep, again. This nap having lasted a few days, they awaked, a second time, and, having eaten, they ventured to crawl to the mouth of their hole, where, pulling away some withered grass and leaves, they peeped out into the open air. After taking a turn or two in the sun, they grew chilly, and went down, again, stopping up the entrance after them. The cold weather returning, they took another long nap, till, at length, Spring being fairly set in, they roused, in earnest, and began to make daily excursions abroad. Their Winter stock of provision being now exhausted, they were for some time reduced to great straits, and obliged to dig for roots, and search for nuts. Their fare improved, as the season advanced, and they made a nest near the bottom of a tree, where they brought up a young family. They never ranged far from home, nor ascended the higher branches of the tree, but passed a great part of their time in sleep, even during the midst of Summer. When Autumn came, they were busily employed in collecting the nuts, acorns, and other fruits that fell from the trees, and laying them up in their storehouse, under ground. One day, as Indur was closely engaged in this occupation, at some distance from his dwelling, he was seized by a wildcat, who, after tormenting him for a time, gave him a gripe, and put him out of his pain.

From one of the smallest and most defenceless of animals, Indur found himself instantly changed into a majestic *elephant*, in a lofty forest of the isle of Ceylon.* Elated with this wonderful advancement in the scale of creation, he stalked along, with conscious dignity, and surveyed, with pleasing wonder, his own form and that of his companions, together with the rich scenery of the ever-verdant woods, which perfumed the air with their spicy odor, and lifted their tall heads to the clouds. Here, fearing no injury, and not desiring to do any, the gigantic herd roamed at large, feeding on the green branches, which they tore down with their trunks, bathing in deep rivers during the heat of the day, and reposing in the depths of the forests, reclined against the massy trunks of trees, by night. It was long, before Indur met with any adventure that could lead him to doubt his security. But, one day, having penetrated into a close entangled thicket, he espied, lurking under the dense covert, a grim tiger, whose eyes flashed rage and fury. Though the tiger was one of the largest of his species, yet his bulk was trifling, compared to that of an elephant, a single foot of which seemed sufficient to crush him ; yet the fierceness and cruelty of his looks, his angry growl,

* A large island in the Indian Ocean, southeast of Hindostan, in Asia ; its situation may easily be seen, by looking on a map of Asia or of the world. The largest and best elephants in the world inhabit its forests.

7*

and grinning teeth, struck some terror into Indur.
There was little time, however, for reflection ;
for, when Indur had advanced a single step, the
tiger, setting up a roar, sprung to meet him, attempting to seize his lifted trunk. Indur was dex-
terous enough to receive him upon one of his tusks,
and, exerting all his strength, threw the tiger to a
great distance ; he was somewhat stunned by the
fall, but, recovering, renewed the assault, with re-
doubled fury.   Indur again, and a third time,
threw him off ; after which the tiger, turning about,
bounded away, into the midst of the thicket.   Indur drew back, and rejoined his companions, with
some abatement in the confidence he had placed
in his size and strength, which had not preserved
him from so dangerous an attack.

Soon after, he joined the rest of the herd, in
an expedition beyond the bounds of the forest, to
make depredations on some fields of maize. They
committed great havoc, devouring part, but tear-
ing up and trampling down much more ; when the
inhabitants, taking the alarm, assembled in great
numbers, and, with fierce shouts and flaming
brands, drove them back to the woods.   Not contented with this, they were resolved to make them
pay for the mischief they had done, by taking
some prisoners.   For this purpose, they enclosed
a large space among the trees with strong posts
and stakes, bringing it to a narrower and narrower
compass, and ending, at last, in a passage only
capable of admitting one elephant, at a time. This
was divided by strong crossbars, which would lift

up and down, into several apartments. They then sent out some tame female elephants, bred to the business, who, approaching the herd of wild ones, inveigled the males to follow them towards the enclosures. Indur was among the first who was decoyed by their artifices ; and, with some others, following heedlessly, he entered the narrowest part of the enclosure, opposite to the passage. Here they stood, awhile, doubting whether they should go further. But the females leading the way, and uttering the cry of invitation, they ventured, at length, to follow. When a sufficient number was in the passage, the bars were let down, by men placed for the purpose, and the elephants were fairly caught in a trap. As soon as they were sensible of their situation, they fell into a fit of rage, and, with all their efforts, endeavored to break through. But the hunters, throwing nooses over them, bound them fast, with strong ropes and chains, to the posts on each side, and thus kept them without food or sleep, for three days ; when, being exhausted with hunger and fatigue, they gave signs of sufficient tameness. They were now let out, one by one, and bound, each of them, to two large tame elephants with riders on their backs, and thus, without resistance, were led away, close prisoners. They were then put into separate stables, and, by proper discipline, were soon rendered quite tame and gentle.

Not long after, Indur, with five more, was sent over from Ceylon, to the continent of India, and sold to one of the princes of the country. He was now trained to all the services in which elephants are there employed ; which were, to carry persons on his back, in a kind of sedan, or litter ; to draw cannon, ships, and other great weights ; to kneel and rise, at command, make obeisance to his lord, and perform all the motions and attitudes he was ordered.   Thus he lived, a long time, well fed and caressed, clothed in costly trappings on days of ceremony, and contributing to the pomp of Eastern royalty.   At length, a war broke out, and Indur came to be employed in a different scene.   After proper training, he was marched, with a number of his fellows, into the field, bearing on his back a small wooden tower, in which were placed some soldiers, with a small field-piece.   They soon came in sight of the enemy, and both sides were drawn up, for battle.   Indur and the rest were urged forwards by their leaders, wondering, at the same time, at the scene in which they were engaged, so contrary to their nature and manners.   In a short time, all was involved in smoke and fire.   The elephants, advancing, soon put to flight those who were drawn up before them ; but their career was stopped by a battery of cannon, which played furiously against them.   Their vast bodies offered a fair mark to the balls, which presently struck down some, and wounded others.   Indur received a shot on one of his tusks, which broke it, and put him to such pain and affright, that, turning about, he ran, with all speed, over the plain ; and, falling in with a body of their own infantry, he burst through, trampling down whole ranks, and filling them with terror and confusion. His leader, having now lost all command over him, and finding him hurtful only to his own party, applied the sharp instrument he carried, to the nape of his neck, and, driving it in, with all his force, pierced his spinal marrow, so that he fell, lifeless, to the ground.

In the next stage of his existence, Indur, to his great surprise, found even the vast bulk of the elephant prodigiously exceeded ; for he was now a *whale*, of the largest species, rolling in the midst of the arctic seas. As he darted along, the lash of his tail made whirlpools in the mighty deep. When he opened his immense jaws, he drew in a flood of brine, which, on rising to the surface, he spouted out again, in a rushing fountain, that rose high in the air, with the noise of a mighty cataract. All the other inhabitants of the ocean seemed as nothing, to him. He swallowed, almost without knowing it, whole shoals of the smaller kinds ; and the larger swiftly turned aside, at his approach. "Now," he cried to himself, " whatever evils may await me, I am certainly secure from the molestations of other animals : for what is the creature that can dare to cope with me, or measure his strength with mine ?" Having said this, he saw, swimming near him, a fish, not a quarter of his length, armed with a dreadful row of teeth. This was a grampus,* which, directly

* This fish abounds in the Northern and Southern seas, the Mediterranean, and the Atlantic Ocean. It grows to the

darting at Indur, fastened on him, and made his great teeth meet in his flesh. Indur roared with pain, and lashed the sea, till it was all in a foam; but could neither reach nor shake off his cruel foe. He rolled over and over, rose and sunk, and exerted all his boasted strength; but to no purpose. At length, the grampus quitted his hold, and left him, not a little mortified with the adventure. This was, however, forgotten, and Indur derived pleasure from his new situation, as he roamed through the boundless fields of ocean, now, diving to its very bottom, now, shooting swiftly to the surface, and sporting with his companions in unwieldy gambols. Having chosen a mate, he took his course with her southwards, and, in due time, brought up two young ones, of whom he was extremely fond. The Summer season having arrived, he more frequently than usual rose to the surface, and, basking in the sunbeams, floated, unmoved, with a large part of his huge body above the waves. As he was thus, one day, enjoying a profound sleep, he was awakened by a sharp instrument, penetrating deep into his back. Instantly he sprung away, with the swiftness of lightning, and, feeling the weapon still sticking, he dived into the recesses of the deep, and staid there, till want of air obliged him to ascend to the surface. Here, another harpoon was plunged into him, the smart of which again made him fly from his un-

length of twenty-five feet, and is a very fierce and voracious animal. It very frequently attacks whales, whence the ancients called it the "tyrant of whales."

seen foes ; but, after a shorter course, he was again compelled to rise, much weakened by the loss of blood, which, gushing in a torrent, tinged the waters as he passed.   Another wound was inflicted, which soon brought him, almost lifeless, to the surface ; and the line, fastened to the first harpoon, being now pulled in, this enormous creature was brought, an unresisting prey, to the side of a ship, where he was soon quite despatched, and then cut to pieces.

The soul of this huge carcass had next a much narrower lodging, for Indur was changed into a *bee*, which, with a great multitude of its young companions, was on flight, in search of a new settlement, their parents having driven them out of the hive, which was unable to contain them all. After a rambling excursion, the queen, by whom all their motions were directed, settled on the branch of a lofty tree.   They all immediately clustered round her, and soon formed a large, black bunch, depending from the bough.   A man presently, planting a ladder, ascended with a beehive, and swept them in.   After they were quietly settled in their new habitation, they were placed on a stand in the garden, along with some other colonies, and left to begin their labors.   Every fine morning, as soon as the sun was up, the greatest part of them sallied forth, and roamed over the garden and the neighboring fields, in search of fresh and fragrant flowers.   They first collected a quantity of gluey matter, with which they lined all the inside of their house.   Then they brought wax, and began to make their cells, building them with the utmost regularity, though it was their first attempt, and they had no teacher. As fast as they were built, some were filled with liquid honey gathered from the nectaries* of flowers ; and, as they filled the cells, they sealed them up with a thin covering of wax. In other cells, the queen bee deposited her eggs, which were to supply a new progeny, for the ensuing year. Nothing could be a more pleasing sight, than to behold, on a sun-shiny day, the insects continually going forth to their labor, while others were as constantly arriving at the mouth of the hole, either with yellow balls of wax under their thighs, or full of the honey, which they had drawn in with their trunks, for the purpose of spouting it out into the cells of the honeycomb. Indur felt much delight in this useful and active way of life, and was always one of the first abroad at the dawn, and latest home in the evening. On rainy and foggy days they staid at home, and employed themselves in finishing their cells, and all the necessary work within doors ; and Indur, though endued with human reason, could not but admire the readiness with which he and the rest formed the most regular plans of work, all corresponding in design and execution, guided by instinct alone.

The end of Autumn now approaching, the bees had filled their combs with honey ; and nothing

* That part of a flower which contains or secretes honey, so called from a Latin word, meaning honey. Its situation varies, in different plants.

more being attainable, abroad, they staid within doors, passing most of their time in sleep. They ate a little of their store, but with great frugality ; and all their meals were made in public, none daring to make free with the common stock, by himself. The owner of the hives now came and took them, one by one, into his hands, that he might judge, by the weight, whether or not they were full of honey. That, in which Indur was, proved to be one of the heaviest ; and he therefore resolved to take its contents. For this purpose, one cold night, when the bees were all fast asleep, the hive was placed over a hole in the ground, in which were put brimstone matches set on fire. The fumes rose into the hive, and soon suffocated most of the bees, and stupified the rest, so that they all fell from the combs. Indur was amongst the dead.

He soon revived, in the form of a young *rabbit*, in a spacious warren. This was like a populous town ; being every where hollowed by burrows, running deep under ground, and each inhabited by one or more families. In the evening, the warren was covered with a vast number of rabbits, old and young, some feeding, others frisking about, and pursuing one another, in wanton sport. At the least alarm, they all hurried into the holes nearest them ; and were, in an instant, safe from enemies, who either could not follow them, at all, or, if they did, were foiled in the chase, by the numerous ways and turnings in the earth, communicating with each other, so as to afford easy means of escape. Indur delighted much in this secure and social life ; and, taking a mate, was soon the father of a numerous offspring. Several of the little ones, however, not being sufficiently careful, fell a prey, either to hawks and crows, who were continually hovering over the warren, or to cats, foxes, and other wild quadrupeds, who used every art to catch them at a distance from their holes. Indur himself ran several hazards. He was once very near being caught by a little dog, trained for the purpose, who kept playing round, for a considerable time, not seeming to attend to the rabbits, till, having got near, he all at once darted into the midst of them. Another time, he received some shot from a sportsman, who lay on the watch, behind a hedge adjoining the warren.

The number of rabbits, here, was so great, that, a hard Winter coming on, which killed most of the vegetables, or buried them deep under the snow, they were reduced to great straits, and many were famished to death. Some turnips and hay, however, which were laid for them, preserved the greater part. The approach of Spring renewed their sport and pleasure ; and Indur was made the father of another family. One night, however, was fatal to them all. As they were sleeping, they were alarmed by the attack of a ferret ;* and,

* A small quadruped, of the weasel tribe. It originally belonged in Africa, but has been introduced into different parts of Europe, and tamed, for the purpose of catching rats and rabbits. It is of a pale, yellowish brown, or cream color, having red and fiery-looking eyes ; it is very irritable. "It

running with great speed to the mouth of their
burrow, to escape it, they were all caught in nets
placed over their holes by the owners of the ferret.   Indur, with the rest, was despatched by a
blow on the back of the neck, and his body was
sent to the nearest market-town.

His next change was into a young *mastiff*,
brought up in a farm-yard.   Having nearly acquired his full size, he was sent, as a present, to
a gentleman in the neighborhood, who wanted a
faithful guard for his house and ground.   Indur
presently attached himself to his master and all
his family, and showed every mark of a noble and
generous nature.   Though fierce as a lion, whenever he thought the persons or properties of his
friends invaded, he was as gentle as a lamb, at
other times, and would patiently suffer any kind
of liberties from those he loved.   He permitted
the children of the house to lug him about, ride
on his back, and use him as roughly as their
little hands were capable of ; never, even when
hurt, showing his displeasure further, than by a
low growl.   He was extremely indulgent to all
the other animals of his species in the yard ; and,
when abroad, would treat the impertinent barking
of little dogs with silent contempt.   Once, indeed,
being provoked beyond bearing, not only by the
noise, but by the snaps of a malicious whelp, he

sleeps, almost continually, and, when awake, immediately begins to search for food ; in a tame state, it is usually fed with
bread and milk ; but its favorite food is the blood of the
smaller animals.''

suddenly seized him in his open mouth ; but, when
the bystanders thought that the poor cur would be
instantly killed, they were equally diverted and
pleased, at seeing Indur go to the side of a muddy
ditch, and drop his antagonist, unhurt, into the
middle of it.

He had, however, more serious conflicts frequently to sustain.   He was accustomed to attend
the servant, on market days, to the neighboring
town ; when it was his office to guard the provision cart, while the man was making his purchases
in the shops.   On these occasions, the boldest
dogs in the street would sometimes make an onset
in a body ; and, while some of them were engag-
ing Indur, others would be mounting the cart, and
pulling down the meat baskets.   Indur had much
ado to defend himself and the baggage, too ; however, he never failed to make some of the assail-
ants pay dearly for their impudence ; and, by his
loud barking, he summoned his human fellow-
servant to his assistance, in time to prevent their
depredations.

At length, his courage was exerted on the most
important service to which it could be applied.
His master, returning home, late, one evening, was
attacked, near his own house, by three armed ruf-
fians.   Indur heard his voice, calling for help, and
instantly flew to his relief.   He seized one of the
villains by the throat, brought him to the ground,
and presently disabled him.   The master, in the
mean time, was keeping off the other two, with a
large stick, but had received several wounds with

a cutlass ; and one of the men had presented a pistol, and was just on the point of firing. At this moment, Indur, leaving his vanquished foe on the ground, rushed forward, and seizing the man's arm, made him drop the pistol. The master took it up ; on which the other robber fled. He now advanced to him with whom Indur was engaged, and fired the pistol at him. The ball broke the man's arm, and then entered the body of Indur, mortally wounding him. He fell, but had the satisfaction of seeing his master remain lord of the field ; and the servants, now coming up, made prisoners of the two wounded robbers. The master threw himself by the side of Indur, and expressed the warmest concern at the accident, which had made him the cause of the death of the faithful animal that had preserved his life. Indur died, licking his hand.

So generous a nature was now no longer to be annexed to a brutal form. Indur, awaking, as it were, from a trance, found himself again in the happy region he had formerly inhabited, and re-commenced the innocent life of a Brachman.

8*

THE NATIVE VILLAGE.

A DRAMA.

SCENE,—*A scattered village, almost hidden with trees. Enter* HARFORD *and* BEAUMONT.

Harford.   THERE is the place.   This is the green on which I played, many a day, with my companions ; there are the tall trees, that I have so often climbed for birdsnests ; and that is the pond, where I used to sail my walnut-shell boats. What a crowd of mixed sensations rush on my mind !   What pleasure, and what regret !   Yes, there is something about our native soil, that affects the mind in a manner, different from every other scene in Nature.

Beaumont. With you, it must be merely the *place ;* for I think you can have no attachments of friendship or affection in it, considering your long absence, and the removal of all your family.

H. No, I have no family connexions, and, indeed, can scarcely be said ever to have had any : for, as you know, I was almost utterly neglected, after the death of my father and mother ; and, while all my elder brothers and sisters were dispersed, to one part or another, and the little remaining property was disposed of, I was left with the poor people who nursed me, to be brought up just as they thought proper ; and the little pen sion, that was paid for me, entirely ceased, after a few years.

B. Then, how were you afterwards supported ?

H. The honest couple, who had the care of me, continued to treat me with the greatest kindness ; and, poor as they were, not only maintained me as a child of their own, but did all in their power to procure me advantages more suited to my birth, than my deserted situation. With the assistance of the worthy clergyman of the parish, they put me to a day-school in the village, clothed me decently, and, being themselves sober, religious persons, took care to keep me from vice. The obligations I am under to them will I hope, never be effaced from my memory, and it is on their account, alone, that I have undertaken this journey.

B. How long did you continue with them ?

H. Till I was thirteen. I then felt an irresistible desire to fight for my country ; and learning, by accident, that a distant relation of our family was a captain of a man-of-war, I took leave of my worthy benefactors, and set off to the seaport, where he lay, the good people furnishing me, in the best manner they were able, with necessaries for the journey. I shall never forget the tenderness, with which they parted with me. It was, if possible, beyond that of the kindest parents. You know my subsequent adventures, from the time of my becoming a midshipman,* to my pres-

* See note on page 57.

ent state of first lieutenant* of our ship.   Though
it is now fifteen years, since my departure, I feel
my affection for these good folks, stronger than
ever, and could not be easy, without taking the
first opportunity of seeing them.

B. It is a great chance, if they are both living.

H. I happened to hear by a young man of the
village, not long since, that they were, but, I believe, much reduced in their circumstances.

B. Whereabouts did they live ?

H. Just at the turning of this corner.   But
what is this ?   I cannot find the house. Yet, I
am sure, I have not forgotten the situation. Surely, it must be pulled down ! Oh ! my dear old
friends, what can have become of you ?

B. You had best ask that little girl.

H. Hark ye, my dear ! do you know one John
Beech, of this place ?

Girl. What, old John Beech ? Oh yes, very
well, and Mary Beech, too.

H. Where do they live ?

G. A little further on, in the lane.

H. Did not they once live hereabouts ?

G. Yes, sir, till farmer Tything pulled the
house down, to make his hop garden.

H. Come with me, and show me the place, and
I will reward you for it.

G. Yes, that I will. (*They walk on.*) There
sir, that low thatched house is the one, and there
is Mary, spinning at the door.

---

* An officer next in rank and command, below the captain.

H. There, my dear ; (*gives her money, and the girl goes away.*) How my heart beats !— Surely, that cannot be my nurse ! Yes, I recollect her, now ; but how very old and sickly she looks.

B. Fifteen years in her life, with care and hardship, must go a great way in breaking her down.

H. (*Going to the cottage door.*) Good morning, good woman ; can you give my companion and me something to drink ? We are very thirsty, with walking, this hot day.

Mary Beech. I have nothing better than water, sir ; but, if you please to accept of that, I will bring you some.

B. Thank you ; we will trouble you for a little.

M. Will you please to walk in, out of the sun, gentlemen ; ours is a very poor house, indeed ; but I will find you a seat to sit down on, while I draw the water.

H. (*to Beaumont.*) The same good creature, as ever ! let us go in.

SCENE II.—*The inside of the cottage. An old man sitting by the hearth.*

B. We have made bold, friend, to trouble your wife for a little water.

John Beech. Sit down, sit down, gentlemen. I would get up to give you my chair, but I have the misfortune to be lame, and am almost blind, too.

H. Lame and blind ! Oh, Beaumont ! (*aside.*)

J. Ay, sir, old age will come on ; and, God knows, we have very little means with which to provide against it.

B. What, have you nothing but your labor to subsist on ?

J. We made that do, sir, as long as we could ; but now, I am hardly capable of doing any thing, and my poor wife can earn very little, by spinning, so we have been forced, at last, to apply to the parish.

H. To the parish ! Well, I hope they consider the services of your better days, and provide for you comfortably.

J. Alas, sir ! I am not much given to complaining ; but, what can a shilling a week do, in these hard times ?

H. Little enough, indeed ! And is that all they allow you ?

J. It is, sir ! and we are not to have that, much longer, for they say we must go to the workhouse.

M. (*entering with the water.*) Here, gentlemen, is the jug, if you can drink out of it ; it is clean.

H. The workhouse, do you say ?

M. Yes, gentlemen, that makes my poor husband so uneasy : to think we should come, in our old days, to die in a workhouse. We have lived better, I assure you ; but we were turned out of our little farm by the great farmer, near the church ; and, since that time, we have been growing poorer and poorer, and weaker and weaker, so that we have nothing with which to help ourselves.

J., (*sobbing.*) To die in a parish workhouse ! I can hardly bear the thoughts of it. But God knows best, and we must submit.

H. But, my good people, have you no children or friends, to assist you ?

J. Our children, sir, are all dead, excepting one, that is settled a long way off, and is as poor as we are.

B. But surely, my friends, such decent people, as you seem to be, must have somebody to protect you.

M. No, sir : we know nobody but our neighbors, and they think the workhouse good enough for the poor.

H. Pray, was there not a family of Harfords, once, in this village ?

J. Yes, sir, a long while ago ; but they are all dead and gone, or else far away from this place.

M. Ay, sir, the youngest of them, and the finest child among them, that I'll say for him, was nursed in our house, when we lived in the old spot, near the green. He was with us, till he was thirteen, and a sweet-behaved boy he was. I loved him as well as ever I did any of my own children.

H. What became of him ?

J. Why, sir, he was a fine, bold-spirited boy, though the best-tempered creature in the world : so, last war, he would be a sailor, and fight the enemy ; and away he went, nothing could stop him ; and we have never heard a word of him, since.

M. Ay, he is dead or killed, I warrant ; for, if he was alive, and in this country, I am sure nothing would keep him from coming to see his poor daddy and mammy, as he used to call us. Many a night have I lain awake, thinking of him !

H. (*to Beaum.*) I can keep concealed no longer !

B. (*to Harf.*) Restrain yourself, a while. Well, my friends, in return for your kindness, I will tell you some news that will please you. This same Harford, Edward Harford,—

M. Ay, that was his name ; my dear Ned ! What of him, sir ? Is he living ?

J. Let the gentleman speak, my dear.

B. Ned Harford is now alive, and well ; he is a lieutenant in the navy, and as brave an officer as any in the service.

J. I hope you do not jest with us, sir.

B. I do not, upon my honor.

M. O, thank God ! thank God ! If I could but see him !

J. Ay, I wish for nothing more, before I die.

H. Here he is, here he is, my dearest, best benefactors ! Here I am, to pay some of the great debt of kindness I owe you. (*Clasps Mary round her neck, and kisses her.*)

M. What, this gentleman, my Ned ! Ay, it is, it is ! I see it, I see it !

J. O, my old eyes ! but I know his **voice,**

now. (*Stretches out his hand, which Harford grasps.*)

H. My good old man ! O, that you could see me as clearly as I do you !

J. Enough, enough ; it is you, and I am contented

M. O, happy day ! O, happy day !

H. Did you think I could ever forget you ?

J. O no, I knew you better ; but what a long while it is, since we parted !

M. Fifteen years, come Whitsuntide.*

H. The first time I set foot in my native country, during all this long interval, was three weeks ago.

J. How good you were, to come to us so soon !

M. What a tall, strong man you have grown ! but you wear the same sweet smile, as ever.

J. I wish I could see him, plainly ; but what signifies it ! he is here, and I hold him by the hand. Where is the other good gentleman ?

B. Here ; very glad to see such worthy people made so happy.

---

* *Whitsuntide,* or *Whitsunday,* a festival, held in commemoration of the descent of the Holy Ghost at the Feast of Pentecost, (see the second chapter of Acts.) It occurs ten days after Ascension-day, or the day kept in commemoration of the Saviour's ascension into heaven ; and fifty days, or seven weeks, from Easter, or the day on which Christians celebrate the resurrection of the Saviour from the dead. The name Whitsuntide is derived from *white,* *Sunday,* and *tide,* or *time,* because it was a remarkable time for baptism, and those who were baptized appeared, in the Ancient Church, clad in white garments.

H. He has been my dearest friend, for a great many years, and I am beholden to him, almost as much as to you two.

M. Indeed! God bless him, and reward him!

H. I am grieved to think what you must have suffered, from hardship and poverty. But that is all at an end; no workhouse, now!

J. God bless you! then I shall be happy, still. But we must not be burdensome to you.

H. Do not talk of that; as long as I have a shilling, it is my duty to give you sixpence of it. Did not you take care of me, when all the world forsook me, and treat me as your own child, when I had no other parent; and shall I ever forsake you, in your old age? Oh, never, never!

M. Ah, you had ever a kind heart of your own. I always used to think our dear Ned would, some time or other, prove a blessing to us.

H. You must leave this poor hut, that cannot protect you from stormy weather, and we must get you a snug cottage, either in this village, or some other.

J. Pray, my dear sir, let us die in this town, as we have always lived in it. And, as to a house, I believe that, where old Richard Carpenter used to live, is empty, if it would not be too good for us.

H. What, the white cottage on the green? I remember it; it is just the thing. You shall remove there, this very week.

M. This is beyond all my hopes and wishes!

H. There, you shall have a little enclosure, to keep a cow in ; and a girl to milk her, and take care of you both ; and a garden, well stocked with herbs and roots ; and a little yard, for pigs and poultry ; and some good new furniture, for your house,—

J. O, too much, too much !

M. What makes me cry so, when so many good things are coming to us ?

H. Who is the landlord of that house ?

J. Our next neighbor, Mr. Wheatfield.

H. I will go and speak about it, immediately, and then return to you again. Come, Beaumont. God bless you both !

J. God in heaven bless you !

M. O, happy day ! O, happy day !

THE HISTORY AND ADVENTURES OF A CAT.

Some days ago, died Grimalkin, the favorite tabby cat of Mrs. Petlove. Her disorder was a shortness of breath, proceeding partly from old age, and partly from fat. As she felt her end approaching, she called her children to her, and, with a good deal of difficulty, spoke as follows :

Before I depart from this world, my children, I mean, if my breath will give me leave, to relate to you the principal events of my life, as the variety of scenes I have gone through may afford you some useful instruction, for avoiding those dangers to which our species are particularly exposed.

Without further preface, then, I was born at a farmhouse, in a village some miles hence ; and, almost as soon as I came into the world, I was very near leaving it, again. My mother had five children ; and, as the frugal people of the house only kept cats to be useful, and were already sufficiently stocked, we were immediately doomed to be drowned ; and, accordingly, a boy was ordered to take us all, and throw us into the horsepond. This commission he performed with the pleasure boys seem often to take in acts of cruelty, and we were presently set a swimming. While we were struggling for life, a little girl, daughter to the farmer, came running to the pond side, and begged, very hard, that she might save one of us, and bring it up for her own. After some dispute, her request was granted ; and the boy, reaching out his arm, took hold of me, who was luckily nearest him, and drew me out, when I was nearly exhausted. I was laid on the grass, and it was some time, before I recovered. The girl then restored me to my mother, who was overjoyed, to get, again, one of her little ones ; and, for fear of another mischance, she took me in her mouth to a dark hole, where she kept me till I could see, and was able to run by her side. As soon as I came to light, again, my little mistress took possession of me, and tended me, very carefully. Her fondness, indeed, was sometimes troublesome, as she pinched my sides with carrying me, and, once or twice, hurt me a good deal, by letting me fall. Soon, however, I became strong and active, and played and gambolled, all day long, to the great delight of my mistress and her companions.

At this time, I had another narrow escape. A man brought into the house a strange dog, who had been taught to worry all the cats that came in his way. My mother skulked away, at his entrance ; but I, thinking, like a little fool as I was, that I was able to protect myself, staid on the floor, growling, and setting up my back, by way of defiance. The dog instantly ran at me, and, before I could get my claws ready, seized me with his mouth, and began to gripe and shake me most terribly. I screamed out, and, fortunately, my mistress was within hearing. She ran to us, but was not able to disengage me. However, a servant, seeing her distress, took a great stick, and gave the dog such a blow on the back, that he was forced to let me go. He had used me so roughly, that I was not able to stand, for some time ; but, by care, and a good constitution, I recovered.

I was now running after every body's heels, by which means, I was one day locked up in the dairy. I was not sorry for this accident, thinking to feast upon the cream, and other good things. But, having climbed up a shelf, to get at a bowl of cream, I unluckily fell backwards, into a large vessel of buttermilk, where I should probably have been drowned, had not the maid heard the noise,

9*

and come to see what was the matter.   She took me out, scolding bitterly at me, and, after making me undergo a severe discipline, at the pump, to clean me, she dismissed me with a good whipping. I took care never to follow her into the dairy, again.

After a while, I began to get into the yard, and my mother took me into the barn, upon a mousing expedition.   I shall never forget the pleasure this gave me.   We sat by a hole, and, presently, out came a mouse, with a brood of young ones.   My mother darted among them, and first demolished the old one, and then pursued the little ones, who ran about, squeaking, in dreadful perplexity.   I now thought it was time for me to do something ; and accordingly ran after a straggler, and soon overtook it.   Oh, how proud was I, as I stood over my trembling captive, and patted him with my paws !   My pride, however, soon met with a check ; for seeing, one day, a large rat, I courage-ously flew at him ; but, instead of turning tail, he gave me such a bite on the nose, that I ran away to my mother, mewing piteously, with my face all bloody and swelled.   For some time, I did not meddle with rats, again ; but, at length, growing stronger and more skilful, I feared neither rats nor any other vermin, and acquired the reputation of an excellent hunter.

I had some other escapes, about this time. Once, I happened to meet with some poisonous food, laid for the rats, and, eating it, I was thrown into a disorder, that was very near killing me.   **At** another time, I chanced to set my foot in a rat-trap, and received so many deep wounds from its teeth, that, though I was loosened, as gently as possible, by the people who heard me cry, I was rendered lame for some weeks after.

After I was a mother, I had the mortification of seeing several broods of my kittens disposed of, in the same manner as my brothers and sisters had been. I shall mention two or three other adventures, in the order I remember them. I was once prowling for birds, along a hedge, at some distance from home, when the Squire's greyhounds came that way, a coursing. As soon as they espied me, they set off, full speed, and, running much faster than I could do, were just at my tail, when I reached a tree, and saved myself, by climbing up it. But a greater danger befell me, on meeting with a parcel of boys, returning from school. They surrounded me, before I was aware of it, and obliged me to take refuge in a tree; but I soon found that a poor defence, against such enemies; for they assembled about it, and threw stones, on all sides, so that I could not avoid receiving many hard blows, one of which brought me, senseless, to the ground. The biggest boy now seized me, and proposed, to the rest, making what he called rare sport with me. This sport was to tie me on a board, and, launching me on a pond, to set some water-dogs at me, who were to duck and half drown me, while I was to defend myself by biting their noses, and scratching their eyes. Already was I bound, and just about to be set a sailing, when the schoolmaster, taking a walk that way, and, seeing the bustle, came up, and obliged the boys to release me, severely reprimanding them for their cruel intentions.

The next remarkable incident of my life was the occasion of my removal from the country. My mistress's brother had a tame linnet, of which he was very fond ; for it would come and light on his shoulders, when he called it, and feed out of his hand ; and it sung well, besides. This bird was usually, either in his cage, or upon a high perch ; but, one day, when he and I were alone in the room together, he unluckily came down on the table, to pick up crumbs. I espied him, and, not being able to resist the temptation, sprung at him, and, catching him in my claws, soon began to devour him. I had almost finished, when his master came into the room ; and, seeing me with the remains of the poor linnet in my mouth, he ran to me, in the greatest fury, and, after chasing me several times round the room, at length caught me. He was proceeding instantly to hang me, when his sister, by many entreaties and tears, persuaded him, after severely whipping me, to forgive me, upon the promise that I should be sent away. Accordingly, the next market-day, I was despatched, in the cart, to a relation of theirs, in this town, who wanted a good cat, as the house was overrun with mice.

In the service of this family, I continued a long time, performing my duty as a mouser, extremely well, so that I was in high esteem. I soon be came acquainted with all the particulars of a town life, and was distinguished for my activity in climbing up walls and houses, and jumping from roof to roof, either in pursuit of prey, or upon gossiping parties with my companions. Once, however, I came very near suffering for my venturesomeness; for, having made a great jump, from one house to another, I lit upon a loose tile, which giving way with me, I fell from a vast height into the street, and should certainly have been killed, had I not fortunately lighted in a dirt cart, whence I escaped, with no other injury, but being half stifled with its contents.

Notwithstanding the danger I had run from killing the linnet, I am sorry to confess, that I was again guilty of a similar offence. I contrived, one night, to leap down from a roof, upon the board of some pigeon-holes, which led to a garret inhabited by those birds. I entered, and, finding them asleep, made sad havoc among all that were within my reach, killing and sucking the blood of about a dozen. I was near paying dearly for this, too; for, on attempting to return, I found it was impossible for me to leap up again, to the place whence I had descended, so that, after several dangerous trials, I was obliged to wait, trembling, in the place where I had committed all these murders, till the owner came up, in the morning, to feed his pigeons. I rushed out between his legs, as soon as the door was opened, and had the good fortune to get safe down stairs, and make my escape through a window, unknown; but never

shall I forget the horrors I felt that night ! Let
my double danger be a warning to you, my children, to control your savage appetites, and, on
no account, to do harm to those creatures, which,
like ourselves, are under the protection of man.
We cats all have a bad name, for treacherous dispositions, in this respect, and, with shame I must
acknowledge, it is but too well merited.

Well,—but my breath begins to fail me, and I
must hasten to a conclusion. I still lived in the
same family, when our present kind mistress,
Mrs. Petlove, having lost a favorite tabby, ad-
vertised a very handsome price for another that
should, as nearly as possible, resemble her dead
darling. My owners, tempted by the offer, carried me, for the good lady's inspection, and I had
the honor of being preferred to a multitude of ri-
vals. I was immediately settled in the comfortable mansion we now inhabit, and had many favors
and indulgences bestowed upon me, such as I
had never before experienced. Among these, I
reckon one of the principal, that of being allowed
to rear all my children, and to see them grow up
in peace and plenty. My adventures, here, have
been few ; for, after the monkey had spitefully
bitten off the last joint of my tail, (for which I
had the satisfaction to see him soundly corrected,) I kept beyond the length of his chain ; and
neither the parrot, nor lap-dogs, ever dared to
molest me. One of the greatest afflictions I have
felt, here, was the stifling of a whole litter of my
kittens, by a fat old lady, a friend of my mistress,

who sat down on the chair, where they lay, and never perceived the mischief she was doing, till she rose, though I pulled her clothes, and used all the means in my power, to show my uneasiness. This misfortune my mistress took to heart almost as much as myself, and the lady has never since entered our doors. Indeed, both I and mine have ever been treated here with the utmost kindness ; perhaps, with too much ; for, to the pampering me with delicacies, together with Mrs. Abigail's frequent washings, I attribute this asthma, which is now putting an end to my life, rather sooner than its natural period. But I know all was meant well ; and, with my last breath, I charge you all to show your gratitude to our worthy mistress, by every return in your power.

And now, my dear children, farewell ; we shall, perhaps, meet again in a land, where there are no dogs to worry us, or boys to torment us. Adieu !

Having thus said, Grimalkin became speechless, and presently departed this life, to the great grief of all the family.

THE LITTLE DOG.

A FABLE.

" WHAT shall I do," said a very little dog, one day, to his mother, " to show my gratitude to our good master, and make myself of some value to him? I cannot draw or carry burdens for him, like the horse; nor give him milk, like the cow; nor lend him my covering, for his clothing, like the sheep; nor produce him eggs, like the poultry; nor catch mice and rats, so well as the cat. I cannot divert him with singing, like the canaries and linnets; nor can I defend him against robbers, like our relation, Towzer. I should not be of use to him, even if I were dead, as the hogs are. I am a poor, insignificant creature, not worth the cost of keeping; and I do not see that I can do a single thing, to entitle me to his regard." So saying, the poor little dog hung down his head, in silent despondency.

"My dear child," replied his mother, "though your abilities are but small, yet a hearty good-will is sufficient to supply all defects. Do but love him, dearly, and prove your love, by all the means in your power, and you will not fail to please him."

The little dog was comforted with this assurance; and, on his master's approach, ran to him, licked his feet, gambolled before him, and, every now and then, stopped, wagging his tail, and looking up to his master with expressions of the most humble and affectionate attachment. The master observed him. Ha! little Fido, said he, you are an honest, good-natured little fellow!—and stooped down to pat his head. Poor Fido was ready to go out of his wits, with joy.

Fido was now his master's constant companion, in his walks, playing and skipping round him, and amusing him, by a thousand sportive tricks. He took care, however, not to be troublesome, by leaping on him with dirty paws ; nor would he follow him into the parlor, unless invited. He also attempted to make himself useful, by a number of little services. He would drive away the sparrows, as they were stealing the chickens' meat ; and would run and bark, with the utmost fury, at any strange pigs, or other animals, that offered to come into the yard. He kept the poultry, geese, and pigs, from straying beyond their bounds, and particularly from doing mischief in the garden. He was always ready to alarm Towzer, if there was any suspicious noise about the house, day or night. If his master pulled off his coat in the field, to help his workmen, as he would sometimes do, Fido always sat by it, and would not suffer either man or beast to touch it. By this means, he came to be considered as a very trusty protector of his master's property.

His master was once confined to his bed, with a dangerous illness. Fido fixed himself at the chamber door, and could not be persuaded to leave it, even to take food ; and, as soon as his master was so far recovered as to sit up, Fido, being admitted into the room, ran up to him with such marks of excessive joy and affection, as would have melted any heart to behold. This circumstance wonderfully endeared him to his master ; and, some time after, he had an oppor-

tunity of doing him a very important service.
One hot day, after dinner, his master was sleeping in a summerhouse, with Fido by his side.
The building was old and crazy ; and the dog,
who was faithfully watching his master, perceived
the walls shake, and pieces of mortar fall from
the ceiling. He comprehended the danger, and
began barking, to awake his master ; and this not
sufficing, he jumped up, and gently bit his finger.
The master, upon this, started up, and had just
time to get out of the door, before the whole
building fell down. Fido, who was behind, got
hurt by some rubbish, which fell upon him ; on
which his master had him taken care of, with the
utmost tenderness, and ever after acknowledged
his obligation to this little animal, as the preserv-
er of his life. Thus his love and fidelity had
their full reward.

MORAL.—The poorest man may repay his obligations to the richest and greatest, by faithful
and affectionate service ; the lowest in rank may
obtain the favor and regard of the Creator himself, by humble gratitude, and steadfast obedience.

THE TWO ROBBERS.

SCENE,—ALEXANDER THE GREAT,* *in his tent.*— GUARDS. *A man, with a fierce countenance, chained and fettered, brought before him.*

Alex. WHAT, art thou the Thracian† robber, of whose exploits I have heard so much ?

---

*Alexander was a celebrated King of Macedonia, who was born about three hundred and fifty-five years before Christ, and died at the age of thirty-two, having reigned twelve years and eight months. His death was, by some, attributed to poison and excessive drinking, and, by others, to a fever. He was famous for the number of battles he fought, and victories that he won, having carried his arms further, and conquered more nations, than any king that preceded him. His victories and success increased his pride to such an extent, that he abandoned himself to pleasure and dissipation. It is related, that, when he was told by the philosopher Anaxarchus, that there was an infinite number of worlds, he wept, to think that it would be impossible for him to conquer all of them, as he had not even conquered one. He burned many cities, squandered immense sums, for the vilest purposes, murdered, in battle and otherwise, millions of people, and brought misery and ruin upon a still greater number. Richly, therefore, has he merited the appellation bestowed upon him in certain ancient annals, " a most mighty robber and murderer." Justly, did an ambassador say to him, " Thou boastest that the only design of thy marching is to extirpate robbers ; and thou thyself art the greatest robber in the world." As justly, when Alexander asked a pirate what right he had to infest the seas, did he answer, " The same that thou hast, to infest the universe ; but, because I do this in a small ship, I am called a robber, and because thou actest the same part with a great fleet, thou art entitled a conqueror."

† The *Thracians* were an order of gladiators, said to be the

Rob. I am a Thracian, and a soldier.

A. A soldier! a thief, a plunderer, an assassin! the pest of the country! I could honor thy courage, but I must detest and punish thy crimes.

R. What have I done, of which *you* can complain?

A. Hast thou not set at defiance my authority, violated the public peace, and passed thy life in injuring the persons and properties of thy fellow subjects?

R. Alexander! I am your captive; I must hear what you please to say, and endure what you please to inflict. But my soul is unconquered; and, if I reply, at all, to your reproaches, I will reply like a free man.

A. Speak freely. Far be it from me, to take advantage of my power, to silence those with whom I deign to converse!

R. I must then answer your question, by another. How have *you* passed your life?

A. Like a hero. Ask Fame, and she will tell you. Among the brave, I have been the bravest; among sovereigns, the noblest; among conquerors, the mightiest.

R. And does not Fame speak of me, too? Was there ever a bolder captain of a more valiant band? Was there ever,—but I scorn to

most fierce and cruel of them all. They were so called, either because they were natives of Thrace, (which was situated in the southeast of Europe,) or wore armor, after the manner of that country. The weapon they used was the falchion, a crooked sword; and they defended themselves with a little round shield.

boast. You yourself know, that I have not been easily subdued.

A. Still, what are you but a *robber* ; a base, dishonest *robber* ?

R. And what is a *conqueror* ? Have not you, too, gone about the earth, like an evil genius, blasting the fair fruits of peace and industry ; plundering, ravaging, killing, without law, without justice, merely to gratify an insatiable lust for dominion ? All that I have done to a single district, with a hundred followers, you have done to whole nations, with a hundred thousand. If I have stripped individuals, you have ruined kings and princes. If I have burned a few hamlets, you have desolated the most flourishing kingdoms and cities of the earth. What is, then, the difference, but that, as you were born a king, and I a private man, you have been able to become a mightier *robber* than I ?

A. But, if I have taken like a king, I have given like a king. If I have subverted empires, I have founded greater. I have cherished arts, commerce, and philosophy.

R. I too, have freely given to the poor, what I took from the rich. I have established order and discipline among the most ferocious of mankind ; and have stretched out my protecting arm over the oppressed. I know, indeed, little of the philosophy you talk of ; but I believe neither you nor I shall ever repay the world, for the mischief we have done it.

A. Leave me. Take off his chains, and use

10*

him well.   (*Exit robber.*)   Are we, then, so much alike ?   Alexander to a robber !   Let me reflect.

PHAETON* JUNIOR, OR, THE GIG DE-MOLISHED.

YE heroes of the upper form,
  Who long for whip and reins,
Come listen to a dismal tale,
  Set forth in dismal strains.

Young *Jehu* was a lad of fame,
  As all the school could tell ;
At cricket,† taw,‡ and prison-bars,§
  He bore away the bell.

---

* *Phaeton* was a fabled son of Phoebus, or the Sun, who is said to have demanded permission of his father, to drive his chariot, for one day.   Phoebus, having before promised to grant whatever request he should make, was forced to comply.   But Phaeton had no sooner received the reins, than he betrayed his ignorance, and incapacity to guide the chariot.   The flying horses became sensible of the confusion of their driver, and immediately departed from the usual track.   Phaeton repented, too late, of his rashness, and Jupiter interfered, struck him with a thunderbolt, and hurled him into the River Po.

† *Cricket.*   A play with bats and ball.

‡ *Taw.*   An old name for marbles.

§ *Prison-bars*, or, more properly, prison-base, is a well-known rural sport, or game, among boys.

Now welcome Whitsuntide* was come,
    And boys, with merry hearts,
Were gone to visit dear mamma,
    And eat her pies and tarts.

As soon as Jehu saw his sire,
    " A boon, a boon !" he cried ;
" O, if I am your darling boy,
    Let me not be denied."

" My darling boy, indeed, you art,"
    The father wise replied ;
" So name the boon ; I promise thee,
    It shall not be denied."

" Then give me, sir, your long lash'd whip,
    And give your gig and pair,
To drive, alone, to yonder town,
    And flourish through the fair."

The father shook his head ; " My son,
    You know not what you ask ;
To drive a gig, in crowded streets,
    Is no such easy task.

" The horses, full of rest and corn,
    Scarce I myself can guide ;
And much I fear, if you attempt,
    Some mischief will betide.

" Then think, dear boy, of something else,
    That 's better worth your wishing,

* See note on page 97.

A bow and quiver, bats and balls,
　　A rod and lines, for fishing.''

But nothing could young Jehu please,
　　Except a touch at driving ;
'T was all in vain, his father found,
　　To spend his breath in striving.

At least attend, rash boy !'' he cried,
　　'' And follow good advice,
Or, in a ditch, both gig and you
　　Will tumble, in a trice.

Spare, spare the whip, hold hard the reins,
　　The steeds go fast enough ;
Keep in the middle, beaten treck,
　　Nor cross the ruts so rough.''

And when within the town you come,
　　Be sure, with special care
Drive clear of sign-posts, booths, and stalls,
　　And monsters of the fair.''

The youth scarce heard his father out,
　　But roared, '' bring out the whisky ;''*
With joy he view'd the rolling wheels,
　　And prancing ponies frisky.

He seized the reins, and up he sprung,
　　And waved the whistling lash ;
' Take care, take care !'' his father cried ;
　　But off he went, slap-dash.

* A light, easy-going carriage.

Who's this light spark ? the horses thought,
  We 'll try your strength, young master !
So o'er the rugged turnpike-road,
  Still faster ran, and faster.

Young Jehu, tottering in his seat,
  Now wished to pull them in ;
But pulling, from so young a hand,
  They valued not a pin.

A drove of grunting pigs, before,
  Filled up the narrow way ;
Dash through the midst the horses drove,
  And made a rueful day ;

For some were trampled under foot,
  Some crushed beneath the wheel ;
Oh ! how the drivers did cry out,
  And how the pigs did squeal !

A farmer's wife, on old blind Ball,
  Went slowly on the road,
With butter, eggs, and cheese, and cream,
  In two large panniers stowed.

Ere Ball could stride the rut, amain*
  The gig came thundering on,
Crash went the pannier, and the dame
  And Ball lay overthrown.

* *Amain.* A word applied to any action or effort, precip-
itately made.

Now, through the town the mettled pair
    Ran, rattling o'er the stones ;
They drove the crowd, from side to side,
    And shook poor Jehu's bones.

When lo ! directly in their course
    A monstrous form appeared ;
A shaggy bear, that stalked and roared,
    On hinder legs upreared.

Sideways they started, at the sight,
    And whisked the gig half round,
Then, cross the crowded market-place,
    They flew with furious bound.

First, o'er a heap of crockery ware,
    The rapid car they whirled ;
And jugs, and mugs, and pots, and pans,
    In fragments wide were hurled.

A booth stood near, with tempting cakes,
    And grocery richly fraught ;
All Birmingham* on t'other side,
    The dazzled optics caught.

With active spring, the nimble steeds
    Rushed through the pass between ;
And scarcely touched ; the car, behind,
    Got through, not quite so clean.

* *Birmingham.*   A large town in England, long celebrat
ed for its hardware manufactures.   The name of the town
is here used for the goods themselves.

For while one wheel one stall engaged,
    Its fellow took the other ;
Dire was the clash ; down fell the booths,
    And made a dreadful pother.

Nuts, oranges, and gingerbread,
    And figs, here rolled around ;
And scissors, knives, and thimbles, there,
    Bestrewed the glittering ground.

The fall of boards, the shouts and cries,
    Urged on the horses faster ;
And, as they flew, at every step
    They caused some new disaster.

Here, lay o'erturned, in woful plight,
    A pedler and his pack ;
There, in a showman's broken box,
    All London went to wreck.

But now the fates decreed to stop
    The ruin of the day,
And make the gig and driver too
    A heavy reckoning pay.

A ditch there lay, both broad and deep,
    Where streams, as black as Styx,*
From every quarter of the town,
    Their muddy currents mix.

* *Styx.* A fabled river of antiquity, whose waters were said to be black ; they were also declared to be so cold and venomous, that they proved fatal to such as tasted them, consumed even iron, and broke all vessels immersed in them.

Down to its brink, in heedless haste,
  The frantic horses flew,
And in the midst, with sudden jerk,
  Their burden overthrew.

The prostrate gig, with desperate force,
  They soon pulled out again,
And, at their heels, in ruin dire,
  Dragged, lumbering, o'er the plain.

Here lay a wheel, the axle there,
  The body there remained,
Till severed, limb from limb, the car
  Nor name nor shape retained.

But Jehu must not be forgot,
  Left floundering in the flood,
With clothes all drenched, and mouth and eyes
  Beplastered o'er with mud.

In piteous case he waded through
  And gained the slippery side,
Where grinning clowns were gathered round,
  To mock his fallen pride.

They led him to a neighboring pump
  To clear his dismal face,
Whence, cold and heartless, home he slunk,
  Involved in sore disgrace.

And many a bill for damage done,
  His father had to pay.
Take warning, youthful drivers, all,
  From Jehu's first essay.

AVERSION SUBDUED.

A DRAMA.

SCENE,—*A road in the Country.* — ARBURY, *and* BELFORD, *walking.*

Belford. PRAY, who is the present possessor of the Brookby estate ?

Arbury. A man of the name of Goodwin.

B. Is he a good neighbor to you ?

A. Far from it ; and I wish he had settled a hundred miles off, rather than come here, to spoil our neighborhood.

B. I am sorry to hear that ; but what is your objection to him ?

A. O, there is nothing in which we agree. In the first place, he is quite of the other side in politics ; and that, you know, is enough to prevent all intimacy.

B. I am not entirely of that opinion ; but what else ?

A. He is no sportsman, and refuses to join in our association for protecting the game. Neither does he choose to be a member of any of our clubs.

B. Has he been asked ?

A. I do not know that he has, directly ; but he might easily propose himself, if he liked it. But he is of a close, unsociable temper, and, I believe, very niggardly.

11

B. How has he shown it ?

A. His style of living is not equal to his fortune ; and I have heard of several instances of his attention to petty economy.

B. Perhaps he spends his money in charity.

A. Not he, I dare say. It was but last week, that a poor fellow, who had lost his all, by a fire, went to him with a subscription paper, in which were the names of all the gentlemen in the neighborhood ; and the only answer, he received, was, that he would consider of it.

B. And did he consider ?

A. I do not know, but I suppose it was only an excuse. Then his predecessor had a park well stocked with deer, and used to make liberal presents of venison to all his neighbors. But this frugal gentleman has sold them all off, and keeps a flock of sheep, instead of them.

B. I do not see much harm in that, now mutton is so dear.

A. To be sure, he has a right to do as he pleases with his park, but that is not the way to be beloved, you know. As to myself, I have reason to think he bears me particular ill-will.

B. Then he is much in the wrong, for I believe you are as free from ill-will to others, as any man living. But how has he shown it, pray ?

A. In twenty instances. He had a horse upon sale, the other day, to which I took a liking, and bid money for it. As soon as he found I wanted it, he sent it off to a fair, in another part of the country. My wife, you know, is passionately fond of cultivating flowers. Riding, lately, by his grounds, she observed something new, and took a great longing for a root or cutting of it. My gardener mentioned her wish to his, (contrary, I own, to my inclination,) and he told his master ; but, instead of obliging her, he charged the gardener, on no account, to touch the plant. A little while ago, I turned off a man, for saucy behavior ; but, as he had lived many years with me, and was a very useful servant, I meant to take him again, upon his submission, which I did not doubt would soon happen. Instead of that, he goes and offers himself to my civil neighbor, who, without deigning to apply to me, even for a character, engages him immediately. In short, he has not the least of a gentleman about him, and I would give any thing to be well rid of him.

B. Nothing, to be sure, can be more unpleasant in the country, than a bad neighbor ; and I am concerned, it is your lot to have one. But there is a man who seems as if he wanted to speak with you. (*A countryman approaches.*)

A. Ah ! it is the poor fellow that was burnt out. Well, Richard, how do you succeed ? what has the subscription produced you ?

Richard. Thank your honor, my losses are nearly all made up.

A. I am very glad of that ; but when I saw the paper, last, it did not reach half way.

R. It did not, sir ; but you may remember asking me, what Mr. Goodwin had done for me,

and I told you he took time to consider of it.
Well, sir; I found, that, the very next day, he
had been at our town, and had made very particular inquiry about me and my losses, among my
neighbors.   When I called upon him, a few days
after, he told me, he was very glad to find that I
bore such a good character, and that the gentlemen, round, had so kindly taken up my case ; and
he would prevent the necessity of my going any
further, for relief.   Upon which he gave me, God
bless him ! a draft upon his banker, for two hundred dollars.

A. Two hundred dollars !

R. Yes, sir.   It has made me quite my own
man again ; and I am now going to purchase a
new cart and team of horses.

A. A noble gift, indeed !   I could never have
thought it.   Well, Richard, I rejoice at your good
fortune.   I am sure, you are much obliged to Mr.
Goodwin.

R. Indeed I am, sir, and to all my good friends.
God bless you ! sir.   (*Goes on.*)

B. Niggardliness, at least, is not this man's
foible.

A. No.   I was mistaken in that point.   I wrong-
ed him, and I am sorry for it.   But what a pity it
is, that men of real generosity should not be amiable in their manners, and as ready to oblige, in
trifles, as in matters of consequence.

B. True ; it is a pity, when that is really the
case.

A. How much less an exertion it would have

been, to have shown some civility about a horse, or a flower root !

B. Apropos* of flowers, there is your gardener carrying a large one in a pot. (*Enter Gardener.*)

A. Now, James, what have you there ?

Gard. A flower, sir, for madam, from Mr. Goodwin's.

A. How did you come by it ?

G. His gardener, sir, sent me word to come for it. We should have had it before, but Mr. Goodwin thought it could not be moved safely.

A. I hope he has more of them.

G. He has only a seedling plant, or two, sir ; but, hearing that madam took a liking to this, he was resolved to send it to her, and a choice thing it is ! I have a note for madam, in my pocket.

A. Well, go on. (*Exit Gardener.*)

B. Methinks, this does not look like deficiency in civility.

A. No ; it is a very polite action ; I cannot deny it, and I am obliged to him for it. Perhaps, indeed, he may feel he owes me a little amends.

B. Possibly. It shows he *can* feel, however.

A. It does. Ha ! there is Yorkshire Tom coming, with a string of horses, from the fair.

---

* *Apropos*, by the way. A word of French origin, pronounced ap-ro-po. It is used to introduce an observation, incidentally made, and which, though appropriate to the occasion, does not strictly belong to the subject immediately under discussion.

11*

I will step up, and speak to him.   Now, Tom!
how have horses gone, at Market-hill ?

Tom.   Dear enough, your honor !

A. How much more did you get for Mr. Goodwin's mare, than I offered him ?

T. Ah, sir ! that was not an animal for your
riding, and Mr. Goodwin well knew it.   You
never saw such a vicious creature.   She liked to
have killed the groom, two or three times.   So I
was ordered to offer her to the mail-coach people,
and get what I could from them.   I might have
sold her to better advantage, if Mr. Goodwin
would have let me, for she was as fine a creature,
to look at, as need be, and quite sound.

A. And was that the true reason, Tom, why
the mare was not sold to me ?

T. It was, indeed, sir.

A. Then I am highly obliged to Mr. Goodwin.
(*Tom rides on.*)   This was handsome behavior,
indeed !

B. Yes, I think it was somewhat more than
politeness ; it was real goodness of heart.

A. It was.   I find I must alter my opinion of
him, and I do it with pleasure.   But, after all, his
conduct, with respect to my servant, is somewhat
unaccountable.

B. I see reason to think so well of him, in relation to most transactions, that I am inclined to
hope he will be acquitted in this matter, too.

A. There the fellow is ; I wonder that he has
my old livery on yet.   (*Ned approaches, pulling
off his hat.*)

Ned. Sir, I was coming to your honor.

A. What can you have to say to me now, Ned ?

N. To ask pardon, sir, for my misbehavior, and beg you to take me again.

A. What ! have you so soon parted with your new master ?

N. Mr. Goodwin never was my master, sir. He only kept me in his house, till I could make up with you, again ; for he said, he was sure you were too honorable a gentleman to turn off an old servant, without good reason, and he hoped you would admit my excuses, after your anger was over.

A. Did he say all that ?

N. Yes, sir ; and he advised me not to delay, any longer, asking your pardon.

A. Well ; go to my house, and I will talk with you, on my return.

B. Now, my friend, what think you of this ?

A. I think more than I can well express. It will be a lesson to me, never to make hasty judgements again.

B. Why, indeed, to have concluded, that such a man had nothing of the gentleman about him, must have been rather hasty.

A. I acknowledge it. But it is the misfortune of these reserved characters, that they are so long in making themselves known ; though, when they are known, they often prove the most truly estimable. I am afraid, even now, that I must be content with esteeming him at a distance.

B. Why so ?

A. You know I am of an open, sociable disposition.

B. Perhaps he is so, too.

A. If he was, surely, we should have been better acquainted, before this time.

B. It may have been prejudice, rather than temper, that has kept you asunder.

A. Possibly so. That vile spirit of party has such a sway in the country, that men of the most liberal dispositions can hardly free themselves from its influence. It poisons all the kindness of society ; and yonder comes an instance of its pernicious effects.

B. Who is he ?

A. A poor schoolmaster, with a large family, in the next market-town, who has lost all his scholars, by his activity on our side, in the last election. I heartily wish it was in my power to do something for him ; for he is a very honest man, though perhaps rather too warm. (*The schoolmaster comes up.*)

A. Now, Mr. Penman, how go things with you ?

Penman. I thank you, sir, they have gone poorly enough, but I hope they are in the way to mend.

A. I am glad to hear it ; but how ?

P. Why, sir, the free-school of Stoke is vacant, and I believe I am likely to get it.

A. Ah ! I wonder at that. I thought it was in the hands of the other party.

P. It is, sir ; but Mr. Goodwin has been so

kind, as to give me a recommendation, and his interest is sufficient to carry it.

A. Mr. Goodwin! you surprise me.

P. I was much surprised, too, sir. He sent for me, of his own accord, (for I should never have thought of asking from *him*, a favor,) and told me, he was sorry a man should be injured in his profession, on account of party, and, as I could not live, comfortably, where I was, he would try to settle me in a better place. So he mentioned the vacancy of Stoke, and offered me letters to the trustees. I was never so affected, in my life, sir. I could hardly speak, to return him thanks. He kept me to dinner, and treated me with the greatest respect. Indeed, I believe there is not a kinder man breathing, than Mr. Goodwin.

A. You have the best reason in the world for saying so, Mr. Penman. What; did he converse familiarly, with you!

P. Quite so sir. We talked a great deal, about party affairs, in this neighborhood ; and he lamented, much, that differences, of this kind, should keep worthy men at a distance from each other. I took the liberty, sir, of mentioning your name. He said, he had not the honor of being acquainted with you ; but that he had a sincere esteem for your character, and should be glad of any occasion to cultivate a friendship with you. For my part, I confess, to my shame, I did not think there could have been such a man, on that side.

A. Well, good morning.

P. Your most obedient, sir. (*He goes.*)

A. (*after some silence,*) Come, my friend, let us go.

B. Whither ?

A. Can you doubt ?   To Mr. Goodwin's, to be sure.   After all that I have heard, can I exist a moment, without acknowledging the injustice I have done him, and soliciting his friendship ?

B. I shall be happy, I am sure, to accompany you, on that errand.   But who is to introduce us ?

A. What is form and ceremony, in a case like this ?   Come ; come.

B. Most willingly.

THE FEMALE CHOICE.

A TALE.

A YOUNG girl, having fatigued herself, one day, with running about the garden, sat herself down, in a pleasant arbor, where she presently fell asleep. During her slumber, she dreamed that two female figures presented themselves before her.   One was loosely habited in a thin robe of pink, with light green trimmings.   Her sash, of silver gauze, flowed to the ground.   Her fair hair fell, in ringlets, down her neck ; and her head-dress consisted of artificial flowers, interwoven with feathers. She held, in one hand, a ball ticket, and, in the other, a fancy dress, all covered with spangles and knots of gay riband.   She advanced, smilingly, to the girl, and, with a familiar air, thus addressed her :

"My dearest Melissa ; I am a kind genius, who have watched you, from your birth, and have joyfully beheld all your beauties expand, till, at length, they have rendered you a companion worthy of me. See what I have brought you. This dress and this ticket will give you free access to all the enchanting delights of my palace. With me, you will pass your days in a perpetual round of ever-varying amusements. Like the gay butterfly, you will have no other business, than to flutter from flower to flower, and spread your charms before admiring spectators. No restraints, no toils, no dull tasks, are to be found, within my happy domains. All is pleasure, life, and good humor. Come then, my dear ! Let me put on you this dress, which will make you quite charming ; and away, away, with me !"

Melissa felt a strong inclination to comply with the call of this inviting nymph ; but first, she thought it would be prudent, at least, to ask her name.

"My name," said she, "is DISSIPATION."

The other female then advanced. She was clothed in a close habit of brown stuff, simply varied with white. She wore her smooth hair under a plain cap. Her whole person was perfectly neat and clean. Her look was serious, but satisfied ; and her air was staid and composed. She held, in one hand, a distaff ; on the opposite arm, hung a work-basket ; and the girdle round her waist was garnished with scissors, knittingneedles, reels, and other implements of female labor. A bunch of keys hung at her side. She thus accosted the sleeping girl :

"Melissa, I am the genius who has ever been the friend and companion of your mother ; and I now offer my protection to you. I have not allurements, like those of my gay rival, with which to tempt you. Instead of spending all your time in amusements, if you enter yourself in my train, you must rise early, and pass the long day in a variety of employments, some of them difficult, some laborious, and all requiring exertion of body or mind. You must dress plainly, live mostly at home, and aim at being useful, rather than shining. But, in return, I will insure you content, even spirits, self-approbation, and the esteem of all who thoroughly know you. If these offers appear to your young mind less inviting, than those of my rival, be assured, however, that they are more real. She has promised much more, than she can ever make good. Perpetual pleasures are no more in the power of Dissipation, than of Vice or Folly, to bestow. Her delights quickly pall, and are inevitably succeeded by languor and disgust. She appears to you under a disguise, and what you see is not her real face. For myself, I shall never seem to you less amiable than I now do, but, on the contrary, you will like me better and better. If I look grave to you, now, you will hear me sing at my work ; and, when work is over, I can dance, too. But I have said enough. It is time for you to choose whom you will follow ; and upon that choice all your happiness depends. If you would know my name, it is HOUSEWIFERY.''

Melissa heard her with more attention, than delight ; and, though overawed by her manner, she could not help turning, again, to take another look at the first speaker. She beheld her still offering her presents, with so bewitching an air, that she felt it scarcely possible to resist ; when, by a fortunate accident, the mask, with which Dissipation's face was so artfully covered, fell off. As soon as Melissa beheld, instead of the smiling features of youth and cheerfulness, a countenance, wan and ghastly with sickness, and soured by fretfulness, she turned away, with horror, and gave her hand, unreluctantly, to her sober and sincere companion.

THE PRICE OF A VICTORY.

GOOD news ! great news ! glorious news ! cried young Oswald, as he entered his father's house. We have gained a complete victory, and have killed, I do not know how many thousands of the enemy ; and we are to have bonfires and illuminations !

And so, said his father, you think that killing a great many thousands of human creatures, is a thing to be very glad about.

12   VIII.

Oswald. No ; I do not quite think so, neither ; but surely, it is right to be glad that our country has gained a great advantage.

Father. No doubt, it is right to wish well to our country, as far as its prosperity can be promoted, without injuring the rest of mankind. But wars are very seldom to the real advantage of any nation ; and when they are ever so useful or necessary, so many dreadful evils attend them, that a humane man will scarcely rejoice in them, if he considers at all on the subject.

O. But, if our enemies would do us a great deal of mischief, and we prevent it by conquering them, have not we a right to be glad of it.

F. Alas ! we are, in general, poor judges, which of the parties has the most mischievous intentions. Commonly, they are both in the wrong, and success will make both of them unjust, and unreasonable. But, putting that out of the question, he, who rejoices in the event of a battle, rejoices in the misery of many thousands of his species ; and the thought of that should make him pause a little. Suppose a surgeon were to come, with a smiling countenance, and tell us, triumphantly, that he had cut off half a dozen legs, to-day. What would you think of him ?

O. I should think him very hard-hearted.

F. And yet those operations are done for the benefit of the sufferers, and by their own desire. But, in a battle, the probability is, that none of those engaged, on either side, have any interest, at all, in the cause they are fighting for, and most of them come there, because they cannot help it. In this battle, that you are so rejoiced about, there have been ten thousand men killed upon the spot, and nearly as many wounded.

O. On both sides ?

F. Yes ; but they are *men*, on both sides. Consider; now, that the ten thousand, sent out of the world on this morning's work, though they are past feeling, themselves, have left, probably, two persons, each, on an average, to lament their loss ; either parents, wives, or children. Here are then twenty thousand people made unhappy, at one stroke, on their account. This, however, is hardly so dreadful to think of, as the condition of the wounded. At the moment we are talking, eight or ten thousand more are lying in agony, torn with shot or gashed with cuts, their wounds festering, some of them hourly to die a most excruciating death, others to linger in torture, weeks and months, and many doomed to drag on a miserable existence, for the rest of their lives, with diseased and mutilated bodies.

O. This is shocking to think of, indeed !

F. When you light your candles, then, this evening, *think what they cost.*

O. But every body else is glad, and all seem to think nothing of these things.

F. True, they do *not* think of them. If they did, I cannot suppose they would be so void of feeling, as to enjoy themselves in merriment, when so many of their fellow-creatures are made miserable. Do you not remember, when poor Dickens

had his leg broken to pieces, by a loaded wagon,
how all the town pitied him ?

O. Yes, very well. I could not sleep, the
night after the accident, for thinking of him.

F. But here are thousands suffering as much
as he did, and we scarcely bestow a single thought
on them.   If any one of these poor creatures
were before our eyes, we should probably feel
much more for him, than we do now for all of
them, together.   Shall I tell you a story of a soldier's fortune, that came to my own knowledge ?

O. Yes, pray do.

F. In the village where I went to school, there
was an honest, industrious weaver and his wife,
who had an only son, named Walter, just arrived
to manhood.   Walter was a good and dutiful lad,
and a clever workman ; so that he was a great
help to his parents.   One day, having gone to the
next market-town, with some work, he met with
a companion, who took him to the alehouse, and
treated him.   As he was coming away, a recruiting sergeant* entered the room, who, seeing Walter to be a likely young fellow, had a great mind
to entrap him.   He persuaded him to sit down,
again, and to take a glass with him ; and kept
him in talk, with fine stories, about a soldier's
life, till Walter became intoxicated, before he was
aware.   The sergeant then clapped a shilling into
his hand, to drink his country's prosperity, and

* *Sergeant.*   An inferior officer in a company, or army,
appointed to teach the soldiers the military exercise, preserve
order among them, &c.

told him he was enlisted. He was kept there, all night, and, next morning, when he had become sober, he was very sorry for what he had done; but he was told, that he could not get off, without paying a large sum, as a punishment. This he knew not how to raise; and, being likewise afraid and ashamed to face his friends, he took the bounty-money,* and marched away with the sergeant, without ever returning home. His poor father and mother, when they heard of the affair, were almost heart-broken; and a young woman in the village, to whom he was engaged to be married, nearly became distracted. Walter sent them a line, from the first stage, to bid them farewell, and comfort them. He joined his regiment, which soon embarked for a foreign clime, where it continued, till the peace. Walter, once or twice, sent word home, of his welfare, but, for the last year, nothing was heard of him.

O. Where was he, then?

F. You shall hear. One Summer's evening, a man, in an old military coat, hobbling on crutches, was seen to enter the village. His countenance was pale and sickly, his cheeks hollow, and his whole appearance bespoke extreme wretchedness. Several people gathered round him, looking earnestly in his face. Among these, a young woman, having gazed at him awhile, cried out, "my Walter!" and fainted away. Walter fell on the ground, beside her. His father and mother, being

* *Bounty-money.* The sum paid, to induce a man to join the public service, in the army or navy.

12*

of the same species, with whom he was frisking and sporting.   He had neither eyes, nor ears, for his old friends of the valley.   All former habits were broken, at once, and he had commenced free partaker of Nature's bounty.   Sylvia came back, crying as much from vexation, as sorrow.   " The little ungrateful thing," said she, " so well as I loved him, and so kindly as I treated him, to desert me, in this way, at last !   But he was always a rover."

"Take care then, Sylvia," said her mother, " how you set your heart upon *rovers* again !"

HOW TO MAKE THE BEST OF IT.

Robinet, a peasant of Lorrain, after a hard day's work, at the next market-town, was returning home, with a basket in his hand.   What a delicious supper shall I have ! said he, to himself. This piece of kid, well stewed down, with my onions sliced, thickened with my meal, and seasoned with my salt and pepper, will make a dish fit for the bishop of the diocese.   Then I have a good piece of a barley loaf, at home, to finish with. How I long to be at it !

A noise in the hedge now attracted his notice, and he espied a squirrel, nimbly running up a tree, and popping into a hole between the branches. Ha ! thought he, what a nice present a nest of young squirrels will be to my little master !   I will try if I can get it. Upon this, he set down his basket in the road, and began to climb up the tree. He had half ascended, when, casting a look at his basket, he saw a dog with his nose in it, ferreting out the piece of kid's flesh. He made all possible speed, down, but the dog was too quick for him, and ran off, with the meat in his mouth. Robinet looked after him. Well, said he, then I must be content with soup-meagre ;* and it is no bad thing, neither !

He travelled on, and came to a little public house, by the road-side, where an acquaintance of his was sitting on a bench, drinking. He invited Robinet to take a draught. Robinet seated himself by his friend, and set his basket on the bench close by him. A tame raven, which was kept at the house, came slily behind him, and, perching on the basket, stole away the bag in which the meal was tied up, and hopped off with it to his hole. Robinet did not perceive the theft, till he was on his way again. He returned to search for his bag, but could hear no tidings of it. Well, says he, my soup will be the thinner, but I will boil a slice of bread with it, and that will do it some good, at least.

He went on, again, and arrived at a little brook, over which was laid a narrow plank. A young woman coming up to pass, at the same time, Robinet gallantly offered her his hand. When she had reached the middle, either through fear, or

* A thin soup, made without meat.

Here, his industry and capacity, in mercantile pursuits, raised him, in a course of years, to greater wealth than he had possessed in his most prosperous days at Genoa ; and his reputation for honor and generosity equalled his fortune.

Among other places, which he frequently visited as a merchant, was the city of Tunis,* at that time in friendship with the Venetians, though hostile to most of the other Italian states, and especially to Genoa. As Uberto was on a visit to one of the first men of that place, at his country house, he saw a young Christian slave at work, in irons, whose appearance excited his attention. The youth seemed oppressed with labor, to which his delicate frame had not been accustomed, and, while he leaned, at intervals, upon the instrument with which he was working, a sigh burst from his full heart, and a tear stole down his cheek. Uberto eyed him with tender compassion, and addressed him, in Italian. The youth eagerly caught the sounds of his native tongue, and, replying to his inquiries, informed him he was a Genoese. "And what is your name, young man ?" said Uberto. "You need not be afraid of confessing to me your birth and condition." "Alas !" he answered, "I fear my captors already suspect enough to demand a large ransom. My father is indeed one of the first men in Genoa. His name is Adorno, and I am his only son." "Adorno !" Uberto checked himself from uttering more, aloud, but, to himself,

---

* In Africa. See a map of that quarter of the world.

he cried, " Thank Heaven ! then I shall be no-bly revenged."

He took leave of the youth, and immediately went to inquire after the corsair captain, who claimed a right in young Adorno, and, having found him, demanded the price of his ransom. He learned that he was considered as a captive of value, and that less than two thousand crowns* would not be accepted. Uberto paid the sum ; and, causing his servant to follow him with a horse and a complete suit of handsome apparel, he re-turned to the youth, who was working, as before, and told him he was free. With his own hands, he took off his fetters, and helped him to change his dress, and mount on horseback. The youth was tempted to think it all a dream, and the flut-ter of emotion almost deprived him of the power of returning thanks to his generous benefactor. He was soon, however, convinced of the reality of his good fortune, by sharing the lodging and table of Uberto.

After a stay, of some days, at Tunis, to despatch the remainder of his business, Uberto departed homewards, accompanied by young Adorno, who, by his pleasing manners, had highly ingratiated himself with him. Uberto kept him, some time, at his house, treating him with all the respect and affection he could have shown the son of his dear-est friend. At length, having a safe opportunity of sending him to Genoa, he gave him a faithful

* A *crown* is a silver coin, about equal, in value, to one dollar and fifteen cents.

13*

servant for a conductor, fitted him out with every convenience, slipped a purse of gold into one hand, and a letter into the other, and thus addressed him :

"My dear youth, I could, with much pleasure, detain you longer in my humble mansion, but I feel your impatience to revisit your friends, and I am sensible, that it would be cruelty to deprive them, longer than is necessary, of the joy they will receive, in recovering you. Deign to accept this provision for your voyage, and deliver this letter to your father. *He* probably may recollect something of me, though you are too young to do so. Farewell ! I shall not soon forget you, and I shall hope you will not forget me." Adorno poured out the effusions of a grateful and affectionate heart, and they parted, with mutual tears and embraces.

The young man had a prosperous voyage, home ; and the transport, with which he was again beheld by his almost heart-broken parents, may more easily be conceived than described. After learning that he had been a captive at Tunis, (for it was supposed that the ship, in which he sailed, had foundered at sea,) "And to whom," said old Adorno, "am I indebted for the inestimable benefit of restoring you to my arms ?" "This letter," said his son, "will inform you." He opened it, and read as follows :

"That son of a vile mechanic, who told you that one day you might repent the scorn with which you treated him, has the satisfaction of seeing his prediction accomplished. For know, proud noble ! that the deliverer of your only son from slavery is,—*the banished Uberto*."

Adorno dropped the letter, and covered his face with his hand, while his son was displaying, in the warmest language of gratitude, the virtues of Uberto, and the truly paternal kindness he had experienced from him. As the debt could not be cancelled, Adorno resolved, if possible, to repay it. He made such powerful intercession with the other nobles, that the sentence pronounced on Uberto was reversed, and full permission given him to return to Genoa. In apprizing him of this event, Adorno expressed his sense of the obligations he lay under to him, acknowledged the genuine nobleness of his character, and requested his friendship. Uberto returned to his country, and closed his days in peace, with the universal esteem of his fellow-citizens.

TRUE HEROISM.

You have read, my Edmund, the stories of Achilles,* and Alexander,† and Charles of Sweden,‡ and have, I doubt not, admired that high

* A Grecian prince, who lived before the Christian era, and is supposed to have died eleven hundred and eighty-four years before Christ.

† A short sketch of Alexander the Great will be found, in a Note, on page 111.

‡ *Charles the Twelfth*, King of Sweden, was born in 1682,

courage which seemed to set them above all sensations of fear, and rendered them capable of the most extraordinary actions. The world calls these men *heroes*; but, before we give them that noble appellation, let us consider what were the motives, which animated them to act and suffer as they did.

The first was a ferocious savage, governed by the passions of anger and revenge, in gratifying which, he disregarded all impulses of duty and humanity. The second was intoxicated with the love of glory, swollen with absurd pride, and enslaved by dissolute pleasures; and, in pursuit of these objects, he reckoned the blood of millions as of no account. The third was unfeeling, obstinate, and tyrannical, and preferred ruining his country, and sacrificing all his faithful followers, to the humiliation of giving up any of his mad projects. *Self,* you see, was the spring of all their conduct; and a *selfish man* can never be a hero. I will give you two examples of genuine heroism, one shown in acting, the other in suffering; and these shall be *true stories,* which is perhaps more than can be said of half that is recorded of Achilles and Alexander.

You have probably heard something of Mr.

and ascended the throne, on the death of his father, in 1697; he died in the thirty-seventh year of his age, having reigned twenty-one years. "His wonderful intrepidity and perseverance, in whatever he undertook; his fortitude, under misfortune; his contempt of danger, and his passion for glory, will forever rank him foremost among military heroes; but no king was ever more lavish of human blood, or ever less consulted the real interests and happiness of his people."

Howard, the reformer of prisons, to whom a monument is erected in St. Paul's church, London. His whole life, almost, was heroism; for he confronted all sorts of dangers, with the sole view of relieving the miseries of his fellow-creatures. When he began to examine the state of prisons, in England, scarcely any, in that country, was free from a very fatal and infectious distemper, called the gaol-fever. Wherever he heard of it, he made a point of seeing the poor sufferers, and often went down into their dungeons, when the keepers themselves would not accompany him. He travelled, several times, over almost the whole of Europe, and even into Asia, in order to gain a knowledge of the state of prisons and hospitals, and point out means for lessening the calamities that prevail in them. He even went into countries where the plague was, that he might learn the best methods of treating that terrible, contagious disease; and he voluntarily exposed himself to perform a strict quarantine, as one suspected of having the infection of the plague, only that he might be thoroughly acquainted with the methods used for the prevention of it. He at length died of a fever, caught in attending upon the sick, on the borders of Crim Tartary,* honored and admired by all Europe, after having greatly contributed to enlighten his own and many other countries, with respect to some of the most important objects of humanity. Such was *Howard*

* *Crim Tartary*, or Crimea, is a peninsula in Asia, situated on the Black Sea. See a map of Asia.

Oswald. No ; I do not quite think so, neither ; but surely, it is right to be glad that our country has gained a great advantage.

Father. No doubt, it is right to wish well to our country, as far as its prosperity can be promoted, without injuring the rest of mankind.   But wars are very seldom to the real advantage of any nation ; and when they are ever so useful or necessary, so many dreadful evils attend them, that a humane man will scarcely rejoice in them, if he considers at all on the subject.

O. But, if our enemies would do us a great deal of mischief, and we prevent it by conquering them, have not we a right to be glad of it.

F. Alas ! we are, in general, poor judges, which of the parties has the most mischievous intentions.   Commonly, they are both in the wrong, and success will make both of them unjust, and unreasonable.   But, putting that out of the question, he, who rejoices in the event of a battle, rejoices in the misery of many thousands of his species ; and the thought of that should make him pause a little.   Suppose a surgeon were to come, with a smiling countenance, and tell us, triumphantly, that he had cut off half a dozen legs, today.   What would you think of him ?

O. I should think him very hard-hearted.

F. And yet those operations are done for the benefit of the sufferers, and by their own desire. But, in a battle, the probability is, that none of those engaged, on either side, have any interest, at all, in the cause they are fighting for, and most of them come there, because they cannot help it. In this battle, that you are so rejoiced about, there have been ten thousand men killed upon the spot, and nearly as many wounded.

O. On both sides ?

F. Yes ; but they are *men*, on both sides. Consider; now, that the ten thousand, sent out of the world on this morning's work, though they are past feeling, themselves, have left, probably, two persons, each, on an average, to lament their loss ; either parents, wives, or children. Here are then twenty thousand people made unhappy, at one stroke, on their account. This, however, is hardly so dreadful to think of, as the condition of the wounded. At the moment we are talking, eight or ten thousand more are lying in agony, torn with shot or gashed with cuts, their wounds festering, some of them hourly to die a most excruciating death, others to linger in torture, weeks and months, and many doomed to drag on a miserable existence, for the rest of their lives, with diseased and mutilated bodies.

O. This is shocking to think of, indeed !

F. When you light your candles, then, this evening, *think what they cost.*

O. But every body else is glad, and all seem to think nothing of these things.

F. True, they do *not* think of them. If they did, I cannot suppose they would be so void of feeling, as to enjoy themselves in merriment, when so many of their fellow-creatures are made miserable. Do you not remember, when poor Dickens had his leg broken to pieces, by a loaded wagon, how all the town pitied him ?

O. Yes, very well. I could not sleep, the night after the accident, for thinking of him.

F. But here are thousands suffering as much as he did, and we scarcely bestow a single thought on them. If any one of these poor creatures were before our eyes, we should probably feel much more for him, than we do now for all of them, together. Shall I tell you a story of a soldier's fortune, that came to my own knowledge ?

O. Yes, pray do.

F. In the village where I went to school, there was an honest, industrious weaver and his wife, who had an only son, named Walter, just arrived to manhood. Walter was a good and dutiful lad, and a clever workman ; so that he was a great help to his parents. One day, having gone to the next market-town, with some work, he met with a companion, who took him to the alehouse, and treated him. As he was coming away, a recruiting sergeant* entered the room, who, seeing Walter to be a likely young fellow, had a great mind to entrap him. He persuaded him to sit down, again, and to take a glass with him ; and kept him in talk, with fine stories, about a soldier's life, till Walter became intoxicated, before he was aware. The sergeant then clapped a shilling into his hand, to drink his country's prosperity, and

* *Sergeant.* An inferior officer in a company, or army, appointed to teach the soldiers the military exercise, preserve order among them, &c.

told him he was enlisted. He was kept there, all night, and, next morning, when he had become sober, he was very sorry for what he had done ; but he was told, that he could not get off, without paying a large sum, as a punishment. This he knew not how to raise ; and, being likewise afraid and ashamed to face his friends, he took the bounty-money,* and marched away with the sergeant, without ever returning home. His poor father and mother, when they heard of the affair, were almost heart-broken ; and a young woman in the village, to whom he was engaged to be married, nearly became distracted. Walter sent them a line, from the first stage, to bid them farewell, and comfort them. He joined his regiment, which soon embarked for a foreign clime, where it continued, till the peace. Walter, once or twice, sent word home, of his welfare, but, for the last year, nothing was heard of him.

O. Where was he, then ?

F. You shall hear. One Summer's evening, a man, in an old military coat, hobbling on crutches, was seen to enter the village. His countenance was pale and sickly, his cheeks hollow, and his whole appearance bespoke extreme wretchedness. Several people gathered round him, looking earnestly in his face. Among these, a young woman, having gazed at him awhile, cried out, " my Walter !" and fainted away. Walter fell on the ground, beside her. His father and mother, being

* *Bounty-money.* The sum paid, to induce a man to join the public service, in the army or navy.

brought by some of the spectators, came and took him in their arms, weeping bitterly. I saw the whole scene, and shall never forget it. At length, the neighbors helped them into the house, where Walter told them the following story.

" At the last great battle, that our troops gained, I was among the first engaged, and received a shot, that broke my thigh. I fell, and, presently after, our regiment was forced to retreat. A squadron of the enemy's horse came galloping down upon us. A trooper making a blow at me with his sabre, as I lay, I lifted up my arm, to save my head, and received a cut, which divided all the sinews at the back of my wrist. Soon after, the enemy were driven back, and came across us again. A horse set his foot on my side, and broke three of my ribs. The action was long and bloody, and the wounded, on both sides, were left on the field, all night. A dreadful night it was to me, you may think ! I had fainted, through loss of blood, and, when I recovered, I was tormented with thirst, and the cold air made my wounds smart, intolerably. About noon, next day, wagons came, to carry away those who remained alive ; and I, with a number of others, was put into one, to be conveyed to the next town. The motion of the carriage was terrible, for my broken bones ; every jolt went to my heart. We were taken to a hospital, which was crowded as full as it could hold ; and we should all have been suffocated, with the heat and stench, had not a fever broke out, which soon thinned our numbers. I took it, and was twice given over, as incurable ; however, I struggled through. But my wounds proved so difficult to heal, that it was almost a twelvemonth, before I could be discharged. A great deal of the bone of my thigh came away, in splinters, and left the limb crooked and useless, as you see. I entirely lost the use of three fingers of my right hand ; and my broken ribs made me spit blood, a long time, and have left a cough and difficulty of breathing, which I believe will bring me to my grave. I was sent home and discharged from the army, and I have begged my way hither, as well as I could. I am told that the peace has left the affairs of my country just as they were, before ; but who will restore me my health and limbs ? I am put on the list as a pensioner, which will support me, if I live to receive it, without being a burden to my friends. That is all that remains for Walter, now !

O. Poor Walter ! What became of him, afterwards ?

F. The wound of his thigh broke out, afresh, and discharged more splinters, after a great deal of pain and fever. As Winter came on, his cough increased. He wasted to a skeleton, and died the next Spring. The young woman, to whom he was to have been married, sat up with him, every night, to the last ; and, soon after his death, she fell into a consumption, and followed him. The old people, deprived of the stay and comfort of their age, sank into despair and poverty, and were taken into the almshouse, where they ended their days.

This was the history of *Walter the Soldier.*
It has been that of thousands more ; and will be
that of many a poor fellow, over whose fate you
are now rejoicing. Such is the *price of a victory.*

THE KID.

ONE bleak day in March, Sylvia, returning from
a visit to the sheepfold, met with a young Kid,
deserted by its dam, on the naked plain. It was
bleating, piteously, and was so benumbed with
the cold, that it could scarcely stand. Sylvia
took it up in her arms, and pressed it close to her
bosom. She hastened home, and, showing her
little fondling to her parents, begged she might
rear it for her own. They consented ; and Sylvia immediately procured a basket full of clean
straw, and made a bed for him on the hearth.
She warmed some milk, and held it to him in a
platter. The poor creature drank it up, eagerly,
and then licked her hand, for more. Sylvia was
delighted. She chafed his slender legs with her
warm hands, and soon saw him jump out of his
basket, and frisk across the room. When full,
he lay down, again, and took a comfortable nap.

The next day, the Kid had a name bestowed
upon him. As he gave tokens of being an excellent jumper, he was called *Capriole.* He was
introduced to all the rest of the family, and the
younger children were allowed to stroke and pat

him ; but Sylvia would let nobody be intimate with him, but herself. The great mastiff was charged never to hurt him, and, indeed, he had no intention to do it.

Within a few days, Capriole followed Sylvia all about the house ; trotted by her side, into the yard ; ran races with her, in the field ; fed out of her hand ; and was a declared pet and favorite.

As the Spring advanced, Sylvia roamed in the fields, and gathered wild flowers, with which she wove garlands, and hung them about her Kid's neck. He could not be kept, however, from munching his finery, when he could reach it with his mouth. He was likewise rather troublesome, in thrusting his nose into the meal-tub and flour-box, and following people into the dairy, and sipping the milk that was set for cream. He now and then had a blow for his intrusion, but his mistress always took his part, and indulged him in every liberty.

Capriole's horns now began to bud, and a little white beard sprouted at the end of his chin. He grew bold enough to put himself in a fighting posture, whenever he was offended. He butted down little Colon, into the dirt ; quarrelled with the geese, for their allowance of corn ; and held many a stout battle with the old turkey-cock. Every body said, Capriole is growing too saucy ; he must be sent away, or taught better manners. But Sylvia still stood his friend, and he repaid her love with many tender caresses.

The farmhouse, where Sylvia lived, was situated in a sweet valley, by the side of a clear stream, bordered with trees. Above the house, rose a sloping meadow, and, beyond that, was an open common, covered with purple heath* and yellow furze.† Further on, at some distance, rose a steep hill, the summit of which was a bare, craggy rock, scarcely accessible to human feet. Capriole, ranging at his pleasure, often got upon the common, and was pleased with browsing the short grass and wild herbs, which grew there.

Still, however, when his mistress came to seek him, he would run, bounding, at her call, and accompany her back to the farm.

One fine Summer's day, Sylvia, after having finished the business of the morning, wanted to play with her Kid ; and, missing him, she went to the side of the common, and called, aloud, Capriole ! Capriole ! expecting to see him come running to her, as usual. No Capriole came. She went on, and on, still calling her Kid, with the most endearing accents, but nothing was to be seen of him. Her heart began to flutter. What has become of him ? Surely, somebody must have stolen him ; or perhaps the neighbor's dogs have worried him. Oh, my poor Capriole ! my dear Capriole ! I shall never see you again ! and Sylvia began to weep.

She still went on, looking wistfully all around, and making the place echo with Capriole, Capri-

* A low shrub.
† A plant, covered with thorns.

ole ! where are you, my Capriole ? till, at length,
she came to the foot of the steep hill. She
climbed up its sides, to get a better view. No
Kid was to be seen. She sat down, and wept,
and wrung her hands. After a while, she fancied
she heard a bleating, like the well-known voice
of her Capriole. She started up, and looked
towards the sound, which seemed a great way
over head. At length, she espied, just on the
edge of a steep crag, her Capriole, peeping over.
She stretched out her hands to him, and began to
call, but with a timid voice, lest, in his impatience
to return to her, he should leap down, and break
his neck. But there was no such danger. Capriole was inhaling the fresh breeze of the mountains, and enjoying, with rapture, the scenes for
which Nature designed him. His bleating was
the expression of joy, and he bestowed not a
thought on his kind mistress, nor paid the least
attention to her call. Sylvia ascended, as high
as she could, towards him, and called, louder and
louder, but all in vain. Capriole leaped from
rock to rock, cropped the fine herbage in the
clefts, and was quite lost in the pleasure of his
new existence.

Poor Sylvia staid, till she was tired, and then
returned, disconsolate, to the farm, to relate her
misfortune. She persuaded her brothers to accompany her back to the hill, and took with her
a slice of white bread and some milk, to tempt
the little wanderer home. But he had mounted
still higher, and had joined a herd of companions,

of the same species, with whom he was frisking and sporting.   He had neither eyes, nor ears, for his old friends of the valley.   All former habits were broken, at once, and he had commenced free partaker of Nature's bounty.   Sylvia came back, crying as much from vexation, as sorrow.   " The little ungrateful thing," said she, " so well as I loved him, and so kindly as I treated him, to desert me, in this way, at last !   But he was always a rover."

"Take care then, Sylvia," said her mother, " how you set your heart upon *rovers* again !"

HOW TO MAKE THE BEST OF IT.

Robinet, a peasant of Lorrain, after a hard day's work, at the next market-town, was returning home, with a basket in his hand.   What a delicious supper shall I have ! said he, to himself. This piece of kid, well stewed down, with my onions sliced, thickened with my meal, and seasoned with my salt and pepper, will make a dish fit for the bishop of the diocese.   Then I have a good piece of a barley loaf, at home, to finish with. How I long to be at it !

A noise in the hedge now attracted his notice, and he espied a squirrel, nimbly running up a tree, and popping into a hole between the branches. Ha ! thought he, what a nice present a nest of young squirrels will be to my little master !   I will try if I can get it. Upon this, he set down his basket in the road, and began to climb up the tree. He had half ascended, when, casting a look at his basket, he saw a dog with his nose in it, ferreting out the piece of kid's flesh. He made all possible speed, down, but the dog was too quick for him, and ran off, with the meat in his mouth. Robinet looked after him. Well, said he, then I must be content with soup-meagre ;* and it is no bad thing, neither !

He travelled on, and came to a little public house, by the road-side, where an acquaintance of his was sitting on a bench, drinking. He invited Robinet to take a draught. Robinet seated himself by his friend, and set his basket on the bench close by him. A tame raven, which was kept at the house, came slily behind him, and, perching on the basket, stole away the bag in which the meal was tied up, and hopped off with it to his hole. Robinet did not perceive the theft, till he was on his way again. He returned to search for his bag, but could hear no tidings of it. Well, says he, my soup will be the thinner, but I will boil a slice of bread with it, and that will do it some good, at least.

He went on, again, and arrived at a little brook, over which was laid a narrow plank. A young woman coming up to pass, at the same time, Robinet gallantly offered her his hand. When she had reached the middle, either through fear, or

---

* A thin soup, made without meat.

sport, she shrieked out, and cried, she was falling. Robinet, hastening to support her with his other hand, let his basket drop into the stream. As soon as she was safe over, he jumped in, and recovered it ; but, when he took it out, he perceived that all the salt was melted, and the pepper washed away. Nothing was now left but the onions. Well ! exclaimed Robinet, then I must sup to-night upon roasted onions and barley-bread. Last night, I had the bread, alone. To-morrow morning, it will be of no consequence, what I have. So saying, he trudged on, singing, as before.

GENEROUS REVENGE.

At the period when the Republic of Genoa* was divided between the factions of the nobles and the people, Uberto, a man of low origin, but of an elevated mind and superior talents, and enriched by commerce, having raised himself to be the head of the popular party, maintained, for a considerable time, a democratical form of government.

The nobles, at length, uniting all their efforts, succeeded in subverting this state of things, and regained their former supremacy. They used their victory with considerable rigor ; and, in particular, having imprisoned Uberto, proceeded

* In Italy. See a map of Europe.

against him as a traitor, and thought they displayed sufficient lenity, in passing a sentence upon him of perpetual banishment, and the confiscation of all his property. Adorno, who was then possessed of the first magistracy, a man, haughty in temper, and proud of ancient nobility, though otherwise not void of generous sentiments, in pronouncing this sentence on Uberto, aggravated its severity, by the insolent terms in which he conveyed it. " You," said he, " the son of a base mechanic, who have dared to trample upon the nobles of Genoa, you, by their clemency, are only doomed to shrink again into the nothing, whence you sprung."

Uberto received his condemnation with respectful submission to the court ; yet, stung by the manner in which it was expressed, he could not forbear saying to Adorno, " that perhaps he might hereafter find cause to repent the language he had used to a man capable of sentiments as elevated as his own." He then made his obeisance, and retired ; and, after taking leave of his friends, embarked in a vessel bound for Naples,* and quitted his native country, without a tear.

He collected some debts due to him in the Neapolitan dominions, and, with the wreck of his fortune, went to settle on one of the islands in the Archipelago,† belonging to the State of Venice.

* In Italy. Look on the map of Europe.

† *Archipelago.* A considerable portion of the Mediterranean Sea is so called ; it is partly in Europe, and partly in Asia. Its principal islands are forty-five in number.

Here, his industry and capacity, in mercantile pursuits, raised him, in a course of years, to greater wealth than he had possessed in his most prosperous days at Genoa ; and his reputation for honor and generosity equalled his fortune.

Among other places, which he frequently visited as a merchant, was the city of Tunis,* at that time in friendship with the Venetians, though hostile to most of the other Italian states, and especially to Genoa. As Uberto was on a visit to one of the first men of that place, at his country house, he saw a young Christian slave at work, in irons, whose appearance excited his attention. The youth seemed oppressed with labor, to which his delicate frame had not been accustomed, and, while he leaned, at intervals, upon the instrument with which he was working, a sigh burst from his full heart, and a tear stole down his cheek. Uberto eyed him with tender compassion, and addressed him, in Italian. The youth eagerly caught the sounds of his native tongue, and, replying to his inquiries, informed him he was a Genoese. " And what is your name, young man ?" said Uberto. " You need not be afraid of confessing to *me* your birth and condition." " Alas !" he answered, " I fear my captors already suspect enough to demand a large ransom. My father is indeed one of the first men in Genoa. His name is Adorno, and I am his only son." " Adorno !" Uberto checked himself from uttering more, aloud, but, to himself,

* In Africa. See a map of that quarter of the world.

he cried, " Thank Heaven ! then I shall be nobly revenged."

He took leave of the youth, and immediately went to inquire after the corsair captain, who claimed a right in young Adorno, and, having found him, demanded the price of his ransom. He learned that he was considered as a captive of value, and that less than two thousand crowns* would not be accepted. Uberto paid the sum ; and, causing his servant to follow him with a horse and a complete suit of handsome apparel, he returned to the youth, who was working, as before, and told him he was free. With his own hands, he took off his fetters, and helped him to change his dress, and mount on horseback. The youth was tempted to think it all a dream, and the flutter of emotion almost deprived him of the power of returning thanks to his generous benefactor. He was soon, however, convinced of the reality of his good fortune, by sharing the lodging and table of Uberto.

After a stay, of some days, at Tunis, to despatch the remainder of his business, Uberto departed homewards, accompanied by young Adorno, who, by his pleasing manners, had highly ingratiated himself with him. Uberto kept him, some time, at his house, treating him with all the respect and affection he could have shown the son of his dearest friend. At length, having a safe opportunity of sending him to Genoa, he gave him a faithful

* A *crown* is a silver coin, about equal, in value, to one dollar and fifteen cents.

servant for a conductor, fitted him out with every convenience, slipped a purse of gold into one hand, and a letter into the other, and thus address-ed him :

" My dear youth, I could, with much pleasure, detain you longer in my humble mansion, but I feel your impatience to revisit your friends, and I am sensible, that it would be cruelty to deprive them, longer than is necessary, of the joy they will receive, in recovering you. Deign to accept this provision for your voyage, and deliver this letter to your father. *He* probably may recollect something of me, though you are too young to do so. Farewell! I shall not soon forget you, and I shall hope you will not forget me." Adorno poured out the effusions of a grateful and affection-ate heart, and they parted, with mutual tears and embraces.

The young man had a prosperous voyage, home ; and the transport, with which he was again beheld by his almost heart-broken parents, may more easily be conceived than described. After learn-ing that he had been a captive at Tunis, (for it was supposed that the ship, in which he sailed, had foundered at sea,) " And to whom," said old Adorno, " am I indebted for the inestimable ben-efit of restoring you to my arms ?" " This let-ter," said his son, " will inform you." He opened it, and read as follows :

" That son of a vile mechanic, who told you that one day you might repent the scorn with which you treated him, has the satisfaction of seeing his prediction accomplished. For know, proud noble! that the deliverer of your only son from slavery is,—*the banished Uberto.*"

Adorno dropped the letter, and covered his face with his hand, while his son was displaying, in the warmest language of gratitude, the virtues of Uberto, and the truly paternal kindness he had experienced from him. As the debt could not be cancelled, Adorno resolved, if possible, to repay it. He made such powerful intercession with the other nobles, that the sentence pronounced on Uberto was reversed, and full permission given him to return to Genoa. In apprizing him of this event, Adorno expressed his sense of the obligations he lay under to him, acknowledged the genuine nobleness of his character, and requested his friendship. Uberto returned to his country, and closed his days in peace, with the universal esteem of his fellow-citizens.

TRUE HEROISM.

You have read, my Edmund, the stories of Achilles,* and Alexander,† and Charles of Sweden,‡ and have, I doubt not, admired that high

* A Grecian prince, who lived before the Christian era, and is supposed to have died eleven hundred and eighty-four years before Christ.

† A short sketch of Alexander the Great will be found, in a Note, on page 111.

‡ *Charles the Twelfth*, King of Sweden, was born in 1682,

courage which seemed to set them above all sensations of fear, and rendered them capable of the most extraordinary actions. The world calls these men *heroes* ; but, before we give them that noble appellation, let us consider what were the motives, which animated them to act and suffer as they did.

The first was a ferocious savage, governed by the passions of anger and revenge, in gratifying which, he disregarded all impulses of duty and humanity. The second was intoxicated with the love of glory, swollen with absurd pride, and enslaved by dissolute pleasures ; and, in pursuit of these objects, he reckoned the blood of millions as of no account. The third was unfeeling, obstinate, and tyrannical, and preferred ruining his country, and sacrificing all his faithful followers, to the humiliation of giving up any of his mad projects. *Self*, you see, was the spring of all their conduct ; and a *selfish man* can never be a hero. I will give you two examples of genuine heroism, one shown in acting, the other in suffering ; and these shall be *true stories*, which is perhaps more than can be said of half that is recorded of Achilles and Alexander.

You have probably heard something of Mr.

and ascended the throne, on the death of his father, in 1697 ; he died in the thirty-seventh year of his age, having reigned twenty-one years. "His wonderful intrepidity and perseverance, in whatever he undertook ; his fortitude, under misfortune ; his contempt of danger, and his passion for glory, will forever rank him foremost among military heroes ; but no king was ever more lavish of human blood, or ever less consulted the real interests and happiness of his people."

Howard, the reformer of prisons, to whom a monument is erected in St. Paul's church, London. His whole life, almost, was heroism; for he confronted all sorts of dangers, with the sole view of relieving the miseries of his fellow-creatures. When he began to examine the state of prisons, in England, scarcely any, in that country, was free from a very fatal and infectious distemper, called the gaol-fever. Wherever he heard of it, he made a point of seeing the poor sufferers, and often went down into their dungeons, when the keepers themselves would not accompany him. He travelled, several times, over almost the whole of Europe, and even into Asia, in order to gain a knowledge of the state of prisons and hospitals, and point out means for lessening the calamities that prevail in them. He even went into countries where the plague was, that he might learn the best methods of treating that terrible, contagious disease; and he voluntarily exposed himself to perform a strict quarantine, as one suspected of having the infection of the plague, only that he might be thoroughly acquainted with the methods used for the prevention of it. He at length died of a fever, caught in attending upon the sick, on the borders of Crim Tartary,* honored and admired by all Europe, after having greatly contributed to enlighten his own and many other countries, with respect to some of the most important objects of humanity. Such was *Howard*

* *Crim Tartary*, or Crimea, is a peninsula in Asia, situated on the Black Sea. See a map of Asia.

the Good ; as great a hero, in preserving mankind, as some of the false heroes, above mentioned, were, in destroying them.

My second hero is a much humbler, but not less genuine, one.

There was a journeyman bricklayer in this town ; an able workman, but a drunken, idle fellow, who spent at the alehouse almost all he earned, and left his wife and children to shift for themselves, as they could. This is, unfortunately, a common case ; and, of all the tyranny and cruelty exercised in the world, I believe that of bad husbands and fathers is by much the most frequent, and the worst.

The family might have starved, but for his eldest son, whom, from a child, the father brought up to help him in his work ; and who was so industrious and attentive, that, being now at the age of thirteen or fourteen, he was able to earn pretty good wages, every cent of which, that he could keep out of his father's hands, he brought to his mother. And, when his brute of a father came home, drunk, cursing and swearing, and in such an ill humor, that his mother and the rest of the children durst not come near him, for fear of a beating, this good lad (Thomas was his name) kept near him, to pacify him, and get him quietly to bed. His mother, therefore, justly looked upon Thomas as the support of the family, and loved him dearly.

It chanced, that one day, Thomas, in climbing up a high ladder, with a load of mortar on his head, missed his hold, and fell down to the bottom, on a heap of bricks and rubbish. The bystanders ran up to him, and found him all bloody, and with his thigh broken, and bent quite under him. They raised him up, and sprinkled water in his face, to recover him from a swoon, in which he had fallen. As soon as he could speak, looking round, with a lamentable tone, he cried, "Oh ! what will become of my poor mother !"

He was carried home. I was present while the surgeon set his thigh. His mother was hanging over him, half distracted. "Do not cry, mother," said he, "I shall get well again, in time." Not a word more, or a groan, escaped him, while the operation lasted.

Thomas was a ragged boy, who could not read nor write ; yet he has always stood on my list of heroes.

THE COST OF A WAR.

You may remember, Oswald, (said Mr. B., to his son,) that I gave you, some time ago, an idea of *the price of a victory*, to the poor souls engaged in it.

I shall not forget it, I assure you, sir, (replied Oswald.)

Father. Very well. I mean now to give you some idea of *the cost of a war*, to the people, among whom it is carried on. This may serve to abate something of the admiration, with which historians are too apt to inspire us, for great warriors and conquerors. You have heard, I doubt not, of Louis the Fourteenth, King of France.

Oswald. O yes!

F. He was entitled by his subjects, Louis the Great,* and was compared by them to the Alexanders† and Cæsars‡ of antiquity ; and with some justice, as to the extent of his power, and the use he made of it. He was the most potent prince of his time ; commanded mighty and victorious armies ; and enlarged the limits of his hereditary dominions. Louis was not naturally a hard-heart-

---

* *Louis the Fourteenth*, styled Louis the Great, was born in 1638, and succeeded to the throne, under the Regency of his mother, Anne of Austria, on the death of his father, in 1643. He died, September 1, 1715, aged seventy-seven years, within four days. His throne was surrounded with splendor, and his reign was adorned by great statesmen and generals, ecclesiastics, and men of literature and science. The internal commotions, which had taken place during the reign of his father, had had the effect of calling forth men of talent and energy, who made the national glory, and the splendor of the King, the object of their exertions ; and the reputation of Louis was the work of his ministers and generals. He was, unfortunately, ignorant, and destitute of settled principles ; and, though he rendered many benefits to the arts and sciences, he was the cause of much injury to his subjects, and to all Europe. He was engaged in five wars, which produced much misery. It has been said, by a French writer, " We may allow him good qualities, but not virtue. The misfortunes of succeeding reigns were, in part, his work ; and he has hardly influenced posterity, except for its ruin."

† See note on page 111.

‡ *Cæsar* was the family name of the first five emperors of Rome, and the surname given to the next seven.

ed man ; but, having been taught, from his cradle, that every thing ought to give way to the interests of his glory, and that this consisted in domineering over his neighbors, and making conquests, he grew to be insensible to all the miseries brought on his own and other people, in pursuit of this noble design, as he thought it. Moreover, he was plunged in dissolute pleasures, and the delights of pomp and splendor, from his youth ; and he was ever surrounded by a tribe of abject flatterers, who made him believe, that he had a full right, in all cases, to do as he pleased. Conquest abroad, and pleasure at home, were, therefore, the chief business of his life.

One evening, his minister, Louvois, came to him, and said, "Sire, it is absolutely necessary to make a desert of the Palatinate."

This is a country in Germany, on the banks of the Rhine, one of the most populous and best cultivated districts in that empire, filled with towns, and villages, and industrious inhabitants.

"I should be sorry to do it," replied the King, "for you know how much odium we acquired, throughout Europe, when a part of it was laid waste, some time ago, under Marshal Turenne."*

* Marshal *Turenne* was born at Sedan, one hundred and thirty-five miles northeast of Paris, (France,) in the year 1611. Whilst reconnoitering a place, to fix a battery, (preparatory to an engagement with the Dutch,) July 27, 1675, he was struck by a cannon ball, fired by the enemy, which killed him on the spot, in the sixty-fourth year of his age. The glory of his many conquests was sullied by his cruel de-

"It cannot be helped, Sire," returned Louvois. "All the damage he did has been repaired,
and the country is as flourishing as ever. If we
leave it in its present state, it will afford quarters to
your Majesty's enemies, and endanger your conquests. It must be entirely ruined ; the good of
the service will not permit it to be otherwise."

"Well, then," answered Louis, "if it must

vastation of the Palatinate. He, however, possessed many
good traits of character. "He preserved," says his biographer, "the reputation of a man of worth, wise and moderate,
because his virtues and great talents, which were his own,
covered weaknesses and faults, which were common to him
with so many other men." Many instances of his honor and
integrity might be mentioned ; but we have room only for the
following. An officer advised him to appropriate to his own
use four hundred thousand livres, (upwards of seventy thousand dollars,) stating, that he could gain it, without the
knowledge of government. He replied, that, as he had often
declined such advantages, he did not intend to alter his conduct, at his age. At another time, a city offered him one
hundred thousand crowns, (about one hundred and fifteen
thousand dollars,) to induce him not to pass, with his army,
through its territory. He refused the sum, saying, "As your
city is not in my proposed line of march, I cannot, in conscience, take your money." In the 'Life of Turenne,' by
Ramsay, will be found the following anecdote, showing how
faithfully he would perform what he promised. "Being attacked, one night, by robbers, near Paris, and stripped of his
money, watch, and rings, he engaged to give them one hundred louis d'ors, (about four hundred and fifty dollars,) if
they would return him a ring, not very costly, but highly
prized by him. The robbers consented, and one of them had
the boldness to go to his house, the next day, and, in the
midst of a large company, to demand, in a whisper, the per-
formance of his promise. Turenne ordered the money to be
paid, and suffered the robber to escape, before he related the
adventure."

be so, you are to give orders accordingly." So saying, he left the cabinet, and went to assist at a magnificent festival, given in honor of his favorite mistress, by one of the princes.

The pitiless Louvois lost no time ; but despatched a courier, that very night, with positive orders to the French generals in the Palatinate, to carry fire and desolation through the whole country ; not to leave a house, nor a tree standing ; and to expel all the inhabitants.

It was the midst of a rigorous Winter.

O. O horrible ! But surely, the generals would not obey such orders.

F. What ! a general disobey the commands of his sovereign ! That would be contrary to every maxim of the *trade.* Right and wrong are no considerations to a military man. He is only to do as he is bid. The French generals, who were upon the spot, and saw, with their own eyes, all that was done, probably felt somewhat like men, on the occasion ; but the sacrifice to their duty, as soldiers, was so much the greater. The commands were peremptory, and they were obeyed, to a tittle. Towns and villages were burnt to the ground ; vineyards and orchards were cut down, and rooted up ; sheep and cattle were killed ; all the fair works of ages were destroyed, in a moment ; and the smiling face of culture was turned to a dreary waste.

The poor inhabitants were driven from their warm and comfortable habitations, into the open fields, to confront all the inclemencies of the sea-

son.   Their furniture was burnt or pillaged, and
nothing was left them, but the clothes on their
backs, and the few necessaries they could carry
with them.   The roads were covered with trembling fugitives, going, they knew not whither;
shivering with cold, and pinched with hunger.
Here, an old man, dropping with fatigue, lay down
to die ; there, a woman, with a newborn infant,
sunk, perishing, on the snow, while her husband
hung over them, in all the horror of despair.

O. Oh! what a scene! Poor creatures!
what became of them, at last ?

F. Such of them, as did not perish on the road,
went to the neighboring towns, where they were
received with all the hospitality that such calami-
tous times could afford ; but they were beggared,
for life.   Meantime, their country, for many a
league round, displayed no other sight, than that
of black, smoking ruins, in the midst of silence
and desolation.

O. I hope, however, that such things do not
often happen in war.

F. Not often, perhaps, to the same extent ; but,
in some degree, they must take place, in every
war.   A village, which would afford a favorable
post to the enemy, is always burnt, without hesitation.   A country, which can no longer be maintained, is cleared of all its provisions and forage,*
before it is abandoned, lest the enemy should have
the advantage of them ; and the poor inhabitants
are left to subsist as they can.   Crops of corn are

* Food for horses, or cattle.

trampled down by armies, in their march, or devoured, while green, as fodder for the horses. Pillage, robbery, and murder, are always going on, in the outskirts of the best disciplined camp. Then, consider what must happen, in every siege. On the first approach of the enemy, all the buildings in the suburbs of a town are demolished, and all the trees in gardens and public walks are cut down, lest they should afford shelter to the besiegers. As the siege goes on, bombs, hot balls, and cannon-shot, are continually flying about, by which the greatest part of a town is ruined, or laid in ashes, and many of the innocent people killed and maimed. If the resistance is obstinate, famine and pestilence are sure to take place ; and, if the garrison holds out to the last, and the town is taken by storm, it is generally given up to be pillaged by the enraged and licentious soldiery.

It would be easy to bring too many examples of cruelty, exercised upon a conquered country, even in very late times, when war is said to be carried on with so much humanity ; but, indeed, how can it be otherwise ? The art of war is essentially that of destruction ; and it is impossible there should be a mild and merciful way of murdering and ruining one's fellow-creatures. Soldiers, as men, are often humane, but war must ever be cruel. Though Homer has filled his ' Iliad'* with the exploits of fighting heroes, yet

* A celebrated poem, describing the Trojan war, composed by *Homer*. For a notice of this celebrated Greek poet, see note on page 64.

14*

he makes Jupiter,* address Mars, the god of war, in terms of the utmost abhorrence.

> " Of all the gods, who tread the spangled skies,
> Thou, most unjust, most odious in eur eyes !
> Inhuman discord is thy dire delight,
> The waste of slaughter, and the rage of fight ;
> No blood, no law, thy fiery temper quells." — *Pope.*

O. Surely, as war is so bad a thing, there might be some way of preventing it.

F. Alas ! I fear mankind have been too long accustomed to it, and it is too agreeable to their bad passions, easily to be laid aside, whatever miseries it may bring upon them. But, in the mean time, let us correct our own ideas of the matter, and no longer lavish admiration upon such a pest of the human race, as a mere *Conqueror*, how brilliant soever his qualities may be.

THE HOG, AND OTHER ANIMALS.

A DEBATE once arose among the animals in a farm-yard, which of them was the most valued by their common master.   After the Horse, the Ox, the Cow, the Sheep, and the Dog, had stated their several pretensions, the Hog took up the discourse.

"It is plain," said he, "that the greatest value must be set upon that animal, which is kept for

* *Jupiter* was the most powerful of all the fabled gods of antiquity, and, being placed at the head of all, was styled ' the god of gods.'

his own sake, without there being expected, from him, any return of use and service. Now, which of you can boast so much, in that respect, as I can?

"As for you, Horse, though you are very well fed and lodged, and have servants to attend upon you, and make you sleek and clean, yet all this is for the sake of your labor. Do I not see you taken out early, every morning, put in chains, or fastened to the shafts of a heavy cart, and not brought back, till noon; when, after a short respite, you are taken to work, again, till late in the evening? I may say just the same to the Ox, except that he works for poorer fare.

"For you, Mrs. Cow, who are so dainty over your chopped straw and grains, you are thought worth keeping only for your milk, which is drained from you, twice a day, to the last drop, while your poor young ones are taken from you, and sent, I know not whither.

"You, poor innocent Sheep, who are turned out to shift for yourselves upon the bare hills, or penned upon the fallows,* with, now and then, a withered turnip, or some musty hay, you pay dearly enough for your keeping, by resigning your warm coat, every year, for want of which, you are liable to perish, on some of the cold nights, before Summer.

"As for the Dog, who prides himself so much on being admitted to our master's table, and made

* Uncultivated grounds.

his companion, that he will scarcely condescend
to reckon himself one of us, he is obliged to do all
the offices of a domestic servant, by day, and to
keep watch, during the night, while we are quietly
asleep.

" In short, you are, all of you, creatures maintained for use ; poor, subservient things, made to
be enslaved or pillaged.   I, on the contrary, have
a warm sty, and plenty of provisions, all at free
cost.   I have nothing to do, but grow fat, and
follow my amusement ; and my master is best
pleased, when he sees me lying at ease in the
sun, or filling my belly."

Thus argued the Hog, and put the rest to silence, by so much logic and rhetoric.   This was
not long before Winter set in.   It proved a very
scarce season for fodder of all kinds ; so that the
farmer began to consider, how he was to main-
tain all his live stock, till Spring.   It will be impossible, (thought he,) to keep them all ; I must
therefore part with those I can best spare.   As
for my horses and working oxen, I shall have
business enough to employ them ; they must be
kept, cost what it will.   My cows will not give
me much milk in the Winter, but they will calve
in the Spring, and be ready for the new grass.   I
must not lose the profit of my dairy.   The sheep,
poor things, will take care of themselves, as long
as there is a bite upon the hills ; and if deep snow
comes, we must do with them as well as we can,
by the help of a few turnips and hay, for I must
have their wool, at shearing time, to make out

my rent. But my hogs will eat me out of house and home, without doing me any good. They must be cooked, that is certain ; and the sooner I get rid of the fat ones, the better.

So saying, he singled out the orator, as one of the prime among them, and sent him to the butcher, the very next day.

THE WANDERER'S RETURN.

It was a delightful evening, about the end of August. The sun, setting in a pure sky, illuminated the tops of the western hills, and tipped the opposite trees with a yellow lustre.

A traveller, with sunburnt cheeks and dusty feet, strong and active, having a knapsack at his back, had gained the summit of a steep ascent, and stood gazing on the plain below.

This was a wide tract of flat, open country, checkered with villages, whose towers and spires peeped above the trees in which they were embosomed. The space between them was chiefly arable* land, from which the husbandmen were busily carrying away the last products of harvest.

A rivulet wound through the plain, its course marked with gray willows. On its banks, were verdant meadows, covered with lowing herds, moving slowly to the milkmaids, who came tripping along, with pails on their heads. A thick

* Fit for tillage and ploughing.

wood clothed the side of a gentle eminence, rising from the water, crowned with the ruins of an ancient castle.

Edward (that was the traveller's name) dropped on one knee, and, clasping his hands, exclaimed, "Welcome, welcome, my dear native land! Many a sweet spot have I seen, since I left thee, but none so sweet as thou! Never has thy dear image been out of my memory ; and, now, with what transport do I retrace all thy charms. O, receive me, again, never more to quit thee!" So saying, he threw himself on the turf, and, having kissed it, rose, and proceeded on his journey.

As he descended into the plain, he overtook a little group of children, merrily walking along the path, and stopping, now and then, to gather berries in the hedge.

"Where are you going, my dears ?" said Edward.

"We are going home," they all replied.

"And where is that ?"

"Why, to Summerton, that town there, among the trees, just before us. Do n't you see it ?"

"I see it, well," answered Edward, the tear standing in his eye.

"And what is your name,—and yours,—and yours ?"

The little innocents told their names. Edward's heart leaped, at the well-known sounds.

"And what is *your* name, my dear ?" said he, to a pretty girl, somewhat older than the rest, who hung back, shyly, and held the hand of a ruddy, white-headed little boy.

"It is Rose Walsingham, and this is my youngest brother, Roger."

"*Walsingham!*" Edward clasped the girl round the neck, and surprised her with two or three very close kisses. He then lifted up little Roger, and hugged him, affectionately. Roger seemed as if he wanted to be set down, again, but Edward told him he would carry him home.

"And can you show me the house you live at, Rose?" said Edward.

"Yes, sir, it is just there, beside the pond, with the great barn before it, and the orchard behind."

"And will you take me home with you, Rose?"

"If you please," answered Rose, hesitatingly.

They walked on. Edward said but little, for his heart was full; but he frequently kissed little Roger.

Coming, at length, to a stile, from which a path led across a little field,—"This is the way to our house," said Rose.

The other children parted. Edward set down Roger, and got over the stile. He still, however, kept hold of the boy's hand. He trembled, and looked wildly around him.

When they approached the house, an old mastiff came running to meet the children. He looked up at Edward, rather sourly, and gave a little growl; when, all at once, his countenance changed; he leaped upon him, licked his hand, wagged his tail, murmured, in a soft voice, and seemed quite overcome with joy. Edward stooped down, patted his head, and cried, "Poor Captain, what, are you alive, yet?" Rose was surprised, that the stranger, and their dog, should know one another.

They all entered the house together. A good-looking, middle-aged woman was busied in preparing articles of cookery, assisted by her grown-up daughter. She spoke to the children, as they came in, and, casting a look of some surprise on Edward, asked him, what his business was.

Edward was some time silent; at length, with a faltering voice, he cried, "Have you forgotten me, mother?"

"Edward! my son Edward!" exclaimed the good woman. And they were instantly locked in each other's arms.

"My brother Edward!" said Mary; and took her turn for an embrace, as soon as her mother gave her room.

"Are you my brother?" said Rose. "That I am," replied Edward, with another kiss. Little Roger looked hard at him, but said nothing.

News of Edward's arrival soon flew across the yard, and in came, from the barn, his father, his next brother, Thomas, and the third, William. The father fell on his neck, and sobbed out his welcome and blessing. Edward had not hands enough for them all to shake.

An aged, white-headed laborer came in, and held out his shrivelled hand. Edward gave it a hearty squeeze. "God bless you," said old Isaac; "this is the best day I have seen, this many a year."

"And where have you been, this long while?" cried the father. "Eight years and more," added the mother.

His elder brother took off his knapsack; and Mary drew him a chair. Edward seated himself, and they all gathered round him. The old dog got within the circle, and lay at his feet.

"O, how glad I am to see you all, again," were Edward's first words. "How well you look, mother! but father has grown thinner. As for the rest, I should have known none of you, unless it were Thomas and old Isaac."

"What a sunburnt face you have! but you look brave and hearty," cried his mother.

"Ay, mother, I have been enough in the sun, I assure you. From seventeen, to five and twenty, I have been a wanderer upon the face of the earth; and I have seen more, in that time, than most men have, in the course of their lives.

"Our young landlord, you know, took such a liking to me at school, that he would have me go with him, on his travels. We went through most of the countries of Europe, and, at last, to Naples, where my poor master took a fever, and died. I never knew what grief was, till then; and I believe, the thoughts of leaving me in a strange country went as much to his heart, as his illness. An intimate acquaintance of his, a rich young West Indian, seeing my distress, engaged me to go with

15   VIII.

him, on a voyage he was about to take to Jamaica. There was not sufficient time before we sailed, for me to come and see you, but I wrote you a letter."

"We never received it," said his father.

"That was a pity," returned Edward; "for you must have concluded, I was either dead, or had forgotten you. Well, we arrived safe in the West Indies, and there I staid, till I had buried that master, too; for young men die fast, in that country. I was very well treated, but I could never like the place; and yet Jamaica is a very fine island, and has many good people in it. But for me, used to see freemen work, cheerfully, along with their masters, to behold nothing but droves of black slaves in the field, toiling in the burning sun, under the constant dread of the lash of hard-hearted task-masters; it was what I could not bring myself to bear; and, though I might have been made an overseer of a plantation, I chose rather to live in a town, and follow some domestic occupation. I could soon have become rich, here; but I fell into a bad state of health, and people were dying, all round me, of the yellow fever; so I collected my little property, and, though a war had broken out, I ventured to embark with it for home.

"The ship was taken and carried into the Havanna, and I lost my all, and my liberty, besides. However, I had the good fortune to ingratiate myself with a Spanish merchant, whom I had known at Jamaica, and he took me with him, to

South America. I visited a great part of that country, and saw those famous gold and silver mines, where the poor natives work, naked, forever shut out from the light of day, in order that the wealth of their unhappy land may go to spread luxury and corruption, throughout the remotest regions of Europe.

"I accompanied my master across the great southern ocean, a voyage of some months, without the sight of any thing, but water and sky. We came to the rich city of Manilla, the capital of the Spanish settlements in those parts. There I had my liberty restored, along with a handsome reward for my services. I went thence to China; and from China to the English settlements in the East Indies, where the sounds of my native tongue made me fancy myself almost at home, again, though still separated by half the globe.

"Here, I saw a delightful country, swarming with industrious inhabitants; some cultivating the land, others employed in manufactures, but of so gentle and effeminate a disposition, that they have always fallen under the yoke of their invaders. Here, I was forced to blush for those, whose avarice and rapacity so often have laid waste this fair land, and brought on it all the horrors of famine and desolation! I have seen human creatures quarrelling, like dogs, for bare bones, thrown upon a dung-hill. I have seen fathers selling their families, for a little rice, and mothers entreating strangers to take their children, for slaves, that they might not die of hunger. In the midst of such scenes, I saw pomp and luxury, of which, our country affords no examples.

" Having remained here, a considerable time, I gladly set my face homewards, and joined a company, who undertook the long and perilous journey to Europe, over land. We crossed vast tracts, both desert and cultivated ; sandy plains, parched with heat and drought, and infested with bands of ferocious plunderers. I have seen a well of muddy water more valued, than ten camel-loads of treasure ; and a few half-naked horsemen strike more terror, than a king, with all his guards. At length, after numberless hardships and dangers, we arrived at civilized Europe, and forgot all we had suffered.

" Afterwards, as I came nearer my native land, I grew more and more impatient to reach it ; and, when I had set foot on it, I was still more restless, till I could see, again, my beloved home.

" Here I am, at last ; happy, in bringing back a sound constitution, and a clear conscience. I have also brought enough of the relics of my honest gains, to furnish a little farm in the neighborhood, where I mean to sit down, and spend my days in the midst of those whom I love better, than all the world besides."

When Edward had finished, kisses and kind shakes of the hand were again repeated, and his mother brought out a large slice of cake, with a bottle of her nicest currant wine, to refresh him, after his day's march. " You are come," said his father, " at a lucky time, for this is our harvest supper. We shall have some of our neighbors, to make merry with us, who will be almost as glad to see you, as we are ; for you were always a favorite among them."

It was not long, before the visiters arrived. The young folks ran to meet them, crying, "Our Edward's come back ! Our Edward's come home : Here he is ! this is he !" and so, without ceremony, they introduced them. "Welcome ! welcome ! God bless you !" sounded on all sides. Edward knew all the elderly ones, at first sight ; but the young people puzzled him, for awhile. At length, he recollected this, to have been his schoolfellow, and that, his companion in driving plough ; and he was not long in finding out his favorite and playfellow, Sally, of the next farmhouse, whom he left a romping girl of fifteen, and now saw a blooming, full-formed young woman of three and twenty. He contrived, in the evening, to get next to her ; and, though she was somewhat reserved, at first, they had pretty well renewed their intimacy, before the company broke up.

"Health to Edward, and a happy settlement among us," was the parting toast. When all were retired, *the Returned Wanderer* went to rest, in the very room in which he was born, having first paid fervent thanks to Heaven, for preserving him to enjoy a blessing, the dearest to his heart.

15*

THE KIDNAPPERS.

Mr. B. was accustomed to read, in the evening, to his young folks, some select story, and then ask them, in turn, what they thought of it. From the reflections they made, on these occasions, he was enabled to form a judgement of their dispositions, and was led to throw in remarks of his own, by which their hearts and understandings might be improved. One night, he read the following narrative from *Churchill's Voyages.*

" In some voyages of discovery, made from Denmark to Greenland, the sailors were instructed to seize some of the natives, by force or stratagem, and bring them away. In consequence of these orders, several Greenlanders were kidnapped, and brought to Denmark. Though they were treated, there, with kindness, the wretched beings were always melancholy, and were observed frequently to turn their faces towards the North, and sigh bitterly. They made several attempts to escape, by putting out to sea in their little canoes, which had been brought with them. One of them had gone as far as thirty leagues from land, before he was overtaken. It was remarked, that this poor man, whenever he met a woman with a child in her arms, used to utter a deep sigh, whence it was conjectured, that he had left a wife and child behind him. They all pined away, one after another, and died, miserably."

Now, Edward, (said Mr. B.,) what is your opinion of this story?

Edward. Poor creatures! I think it was very barbarous, to take them from home.

Mr. B. It was, indeed.

E. Have civilized nations any right to behave so, to savages?

Mr. B. I think you may very readily answer that question, yourself. Suppose you were a savage; what would be your opinion?

E. I dare say, I should think it very wrong. But can savages think about right and wrong, as we do?

Mr. B. Why not? are they not *men*?

E. Yes; but not like civilized men, surely!

Mr. B. I know no important difference, between ourselves and those people, we are pleased to call savage, but in the degree of knowledge and virtue possessed by each. And I believe many individuals among the Greenlanders, as well as other unpolished people, exceed, in these respects, many among us. In the present case, I am sure the Danish sailors showed themselves the greater savages.

E. But what did they take away the Greenlanders for?

Mr. B. The pretence was, that they might be instructed in a Christian country, and then sent back, to civilize their countrymen.

E. And was not that a good thing?

Mr. B. Certainly, if it were done by proper means; but to attempt it by an act of violence

and injustice could not be right ; for they could
teach them nothing so good, as their example was
bad ; and the poor people were not likely to learn,
willingly, from those who had begun with injuring
them so cruelly.

   E. I remember Captain Cook* brought over
somebody from Otaheite ;† and poor Lee Boo‡

* For a notice of this distinguished circumnavigator, see
the first volume of ' Pursuit of Knowledge under Difficulties,' edited by Rev. Dr. Wayland, which forms a part of
the larger series of ' THE SCHOOL LIBRARY.'

  † *Otaheite,* one of the Society Islands, in the South Pa-
cific Ocean. It was discovered by Captain Wallis, in 1767,
who called it George the Third's Island. It was visited by
Captain Cook, in 1769, and twice, subsequently. It is now
called Tahiti.

  ‡ Prince *Lee Boo* was a native of one of the Pelew Islands.
These islands were first made known to Europeans, by Captain Henry Wilson, who was shipwrecked there, on the night
between the ninth and tenth of August, 1783. He found "that
the natives were simple in their manners, delicate in their
sentiments, friendly in their disposition, and, in short, a people that did honor to the human race." The Natives were
of a deep copper color, and went naked. The astonishment
they manifested, on seeing Captain Wilson and his men, satisfactorily proved they had never before seen a white man.
The clothes of the strangers perplexed them, very much ; they,
at first, considering them as part of their bodies. When Captain Wilson's brother waited upon the King, he accidentally
took off his hat, at which much astonishment was manifested
by the spectators, they thinking that it was part of his head.
Many things, which, to those conversant with the manners
and customs of civilized life, alone, would appear very strange,
are recorded of these people ; but we have not room to state
them, here. So favorable an opinion did the King entertain
of Captain Wilson and his companions, and such implicit
confidence did he place in them, that, when they left, he per-

was brought here, from the Pelew Islands. But I believe they both came of their own accord.

Mr. B. They did. And it is a great proof of a better way of thinking, among modern voyagers, than former ones, that they do not consider it as justifiable to use violence, even for the supposed benefit of the people they visit.

E. I have read of taking possession of a newly-discovered country, by setting up the nation's standard, or some such ceremony, though it was full of inhabitants.

Mr. B. Such was formerly the custom ; and a more impudent mockery of all right and justice cannot be conceived. Yet this, I am sorry to say, is the title by which European nations claim the greater part of their foreign settlements.

E. And might not the Natives drive them out, again, if they were able.

Mr. B. I am sure I do not know why they might not ; *for force can never give right.*

Now, Harry, tell me what *you* think of the story.

Harry. I think it very strange, that people should want to go back to such a cold, dismal place, as Greenland.

Mr. B. Why, what country do you love best, in all the world ?

H. Our own, to be sure.

mitted his second son, Lee Boo, to go with them to England, where he unfortunately died of smallpox, in December, 1784. A monument was erected to his memory, in the churchyard at Rotherhithe, a town, situated a mile and a half east of London bridge.

Mr. B. But this is by no means the warmest
and finest country.

H. Still, it is my own, native country, where
you, and mamma, and all my friends, live.   Besides, it is a very pleasant country, too.

Mr. B. As to your first reason, you must be
sensible, that the Greenlander can say just the
same ; and the poor fellow, who left a wife and
children behind, must have had the strongest of all
ties to make him wish to return.   Do you think
I should be easy, to be separated from all of you ?

H. No, sir, and neither should we be easy, I
am sure.

Mr. B. Home, my dear, wherever it be, is
the spot towards which a good heart is the most
strongly drawn.

> " Home, home, sweet, sweet home,
> Search all the world over,
> There 's no place like home !' "

Then, as for the pleasantness of a place, that all
depends upon habit.   The Greenlander, being
accustomed to the way of living, and all the objects, of his own country, could not enjoy any
other, so well.   He loved whale fat and seal, as
well as you do pudding and beef.   He thought
rowing his little boat, amid the boisterous waves,
pleasanter employment, than driving a plough or
a cart.   He protected himself against the Winter's
cold, by warm clothing ; and the long night of
many weeks, which you would think so gloomy,
was to him a season of ease and festivity, in his
habitation under ground.   It is a very kind and

wise dispensation of Providence, that every part of the world is rendered the most agreeable to those who live in it.

Now, little Mary, what have you to say ?

Mary. I have only to say, that, if they tried to carry me away from home, I would beat them.

Mr. B. That is right, my girl ! stand up for yourself. Let nobody run away with you, *against your will.*

M. That I will not.

THE GAIN OF A LOSS.

PHILANDER held a high public station, which obliged him to live in a style of show and expense. He kept much company ; made frequent entertainments, and brought up a family of several daughters, in all the luxurious elegance, which his situation and prospects seemed to justify. His wife had balls and parties, at their own house, and frequented all the places of fashionable amusement.

After some years, passed in this manner, a sudden change of affairs threw Philander out of his employment, and at once ruined all his plans of future advancement. Though his place had been lucrative, the expense, it led him into, more than equalled the profits ; so that, instead of saving any thing, he had involved himself considerably in debt. His creditors, on hearing of his reverse of fortune, became so importunate,

that, in order to satisfy them, he was compelled to
sell a moderate paternal estate, in a distant country, reserving nothing out of it, but one small farm.
Philander had strength of mind sufficient to
enable him, at once, to decide on the best plan to
be followed, in his new circumstances ; instead,
therefore, of wasting his time and remaining property, in fruitless attempts to interest his town friends
in his favor, he sold off his fine furniture, and,
without delay, carried down his whole family to
the little spot, he could still call his own, where
he commenced a life of industry and strict frugality, in the capacity of a small farmer.   It was
long, before the female part of his household could
accommodate themselves to a mode of living, so
new to them, and so destitute of all that they had
been accustomed to regard as essential to their
very existence.   At length, however, mutual affection, and natural good sense, and, above all,
necessity, brought them to acquiesce, tolerably, in
their situation, and to engage, earnestly, in its duties.   Occasional regrets, however, could not but
arise ; and the silent sigh would tell whither their
thoughts were fled.

Philander perceived it, but took care never to
imbitter their feelings by harsh chidings, or untime-
ly admonitions.   But, on the first anniversary of
their taking possession of the farmhouse, he assembled them under a spreading tree, that grew
before their little garden, and, while the Summer's
sun gilded all the objects around, he thus addressed
them :

" My dear partners in every fortune, if the revolution of a year has had the effect upon your mind, that it has upon mine, I may congratulate you, on our condition. I am now able, with a firm tone, to ask myself, What have I lost? and I feel so much more to be pleased with, than to regret, that the question gives me rather comfort, than sorrow. Look at yon splendid luminary, and tell me, if its gradual appearance, above the horizon, on a fine morning, shedding light and joy over the wide creation, be not a grander, as well as a more heart-cheering spectacle, than that of the most magnificent saloon, illuminated with dazzling lustres. Is not the spirit of the wholesome breeze, fresh from the mountain, and perfumed with wild-flowers, infinitely more invigorating to the senses, than the air of the crowded drawingroom, loaded with scented powder and essences? Did we relish, so well, the disguised dishes, with which a French cook strove to whet our sickly appetites, as we do our draught of new milk, our homemade loaf, and the other articles of our simple fare? Was our sleep so sweet, after midnight suppers, and the long vigils of cards, as it is, now that early rising and the exercises of the day prepare us for closing our eyes, as soon as night has covered every thing with her friendly veil? Shall we complain that our clothes, at present, only answer the purpose of keeping us warm, when we recollect all the care and pains it cost us, to keep pace with the fashion, and the mortification we underwent, at being outshone by our superiors in fortune?

Did not the vexation of insolent and unfaithful servants overbalance the trouble we now find, in waiting on ourselves?

" We may regret the loss of society ; but, alas ! what was the society of a crowd of visiters, who regarded us merely as the keepers of a place of public resort, and whom we visited with similar sensations ? If we formerly could command leisure, to cultivate our minds, and acquire polite accomplishments, did we, in reality, apply much leisure to these purposes ; and is not our time, now, occupied more to our satisfaction, by employments, of which we cannot doubt the usefulness ? Not to say, that the moral virtues, we are now called upon to exercise, afford the truest cultivation to our minds.

" What then have we lost ? In improved health, the charms of a beautiful country, a decent supply of all real wants, and the love and kind offices of each other, do not we still possess enough for worldly happiness ? We have lost, indeed, a certain rank and station in life ; but have we not acquired another, as truly respectable ? We are debarred the prospects of future advancement ; but, if our present condition is a good one, why need we lament, that it is likely to be lasting ? The next anniversary will find us more in harmony with our situation, than even the present. Look forward, then, cheerily. The storm is past. We have been shipwrecked, but we have only exchanged a cumbrous vessel for a light pinnace, and we are again on our course. Much of our cargo has been thrown overboard, but no one loses what he does not miss."

Thus saying, Philander tenderly embraced his wife and daughters. The tear stood in their eyes, but consolation beamed on their hearts.

PROVIDENCE ; OR, THE SHIPWRECK.

It was a dreadful storm. The wind, blowing full upon the seashore, rolled tremendous waves on the beach, while the half-sunk rocks, at the entrance of the bay, were enveloped in a mist of white foam. A ship appeared in the offing,* driving, impetuously, under her bare poles,† to land ; now, tilting aloft, on the surging waves, now, plunging into the intervening hollows. Presently, she rushed among the rocks, and there stuck, the billows beating over her deck, and dashing against her shattered rigging.

" Mercy ! mercy !" exclaimed an ancient Solitary,‡ as he viewed, from a cliff, the dismal scene. It was in vain. The ship fell on her side, and was seen no more.

Soon, however, a small, dark object appeared coming from the rocks, towards the shore ; at

* *Offing*, out at sea ; or, at a distance from the shore.

† *Bare poles*, without any sails set. In very violent storms, the sails are all taken in, or closely reefed to the mast, and the vessel is then said to be scudding *under bare poles.*

‡ A hermit ; one living alone, and retired from the world.

first, dimly descried, through the foam, then seen, quite plainly, as it rode on the summit of a wave, then, for a time, totally lost. It approached, and showed itself to be a boat, with men in it, rowing for their lives. The Solitary hastened to the beach, and, in all the agonizing vicissitudes of hope and fear, watched its advance. At length, after the most imminent hazards, the boat was thrown, violently, on the shore, and the dripping, half-dead mariners crawled to dry land.

"Heaven be praised!" cried the Solitary ; "what a providential escape!" He led the poor men to his cell, where, kindling a good fire, and bringing out his little store of provision, he restored them to health and spirits. "And are you six men the only ones saved ?" said he.

"That we are," answered one of them. "Threescore and fifteen men, women, and children, were in the ship, when she struck. You may think what a clamor and confusion there was ; women clinging to their husband's necks, and children hanging about their clothes, all shrieking, crying, and praying ! There was no time to be lost. We lowered the small boat, in a twinkling ; jumped in, without staying for our Captain, who was fool enough to be minding the passengers ; cut the rope, and pushed away, just time enough to be clear of the ship, as she went down : and here we are, all alive, and merry !" An oath concluded his speech.

The Solitary was shocked, and could not help secretly wishing, that it had pleased Providence to save some of the innocent passengers, rather than these reprobates.

The sailors, having procured what they could, departed, scarcely thanking their benefactor, and marched up the country. Night came on. They descried a light, at some distance, and made up to it. It proceeded from the window of a good-looking house, surrounded with a farm-yard and garden. They knocked at the door, and, in a supplicating tone, made known their distress, and begged relief. They were admitted, and treated with compassion and hospitality. In the house, were the mistress, her children, and women-servants, an old man, and a boy; the master was abroad. The sailors, sitting round the kitchen fire, whispered to each other, that here was an opportunity of making a booty, that would amply compensate for the loss of clothes and wages. They settled their plan; and, on the old man's coming with logs to the fire, one of them broke his scull with the poker, and laid him dead. Another took up a knife, which had been brought with the loaf and cheese, and, running after the boy, who was making his escape out of the house, stabbed him to the heart. The rest locked the doors, and, after tying all the women and children, began to ransack the house. One of the children continuing to make loud exclamations, a fellow went and strangled it.

They had nearly finished packing up such of the most valuable things as they could carry off, when the master of the house came home. He

16*

was a smuggler,* as well as a farmer, and had just returned from an expedition, leaving his companions, with their goods, at a neighboring public-house. Surprised, at finding the doors locked, and at seeing lights moving about in the chambers, he suspected something was wrong; and, upon listening, he heard strange voices, and saw some of the sailors through the windows. He hastened back to his companions, and brought them with him, just as the robbers opened the door, and were coming out with their pillage, having first set fire to the house, in order to conceal what they had done. The smuggler and his friends discharged their blunderbusses in the midst of them, and then, rushing forwards, seized the survivors, and secured them. Perceiving flames in the house, they ran, and extinguished them. The villains were next day led to prison, amidst the deprecations of the neighborhood.

The good Solitary, on hearing of the event, at first exclaimed, " what a wonderful interference of Providence, to punish guilt and protect innocence !" Pausing, awhile, he added, " Yet, had Providence thought fit to drown these sailors, in their passage from the ship, where they left so many better people to perish, the lives of three innocent persons would have been saved, and these wretches would have died, without such accumulated guilt and ignominy. On the other hand, had the master of the house been at home,

* *Smuggler*, one who brings goods into, or carries them out of, the country, in a way forbidden by law.

instead of following a lawless and desperate trade, he would, perhaps, have perished, with all his family, and the villains have escaped with their booty. What am I to think of all this ?" Thus pensive and perplexed, he laid him down to rest, and, after some time spent in gloomy reflections, fell asleep.

In his dream, he fancied himself seated on the top of a high mountain, where he was accosted by a venerable figure, in long white garments, who asked him the cause of the melancholy, expressed on his countenance.

"It is," said he, "because I am unable to reconcile the decrees of Providence, with my ideas of wisdom and justice." "That," replied the Stranger, "is probably because thy notions of Providence are narrow and erroneous. Thou seekest it in *particular events*, and dost not raise thy survey to the *great whole*. Every occurrence in the universe is *providential*, because it is the consequence of those laws, which Divine Wisdom has established, as most productive of the general good. But to select individual facts, as more directed by the hand of Providence than others, because we think we see a particular good purpose answered by them, is an infallible inlet to error and superstition. Follow me to the edge of this cliff." He seemed to follow.

"Now, look down," said the Stranger, "and tell me what thou seest." "I see," replied the Solitary, "a hawk, darting amidst a flock of small birds, one of which he has caught, while the oth-

was a smuggler,* as well as a farmer, and had just
returned from an expedition, leaving his companions, with their goods, at a neighboring public-
house. Surprised, at finding the doors locked,
and at seeing lights moving about in the chambers,
he suspected something was wrong ; and, upon
listening, he heard strange voices, and saw some
of the sailors through the windows. He hastened
back to his companions, and brought them with
him, just as the robbers opened the door, and were
coming out with their pillage, having first set fire
to the house, in order to conceal what they had
done. The smuggler and his friends discharged
their blunderbusses in the midst of them, and then,
rushing forwards, seized the survivors, and secured
them. Perceiving flames in the house, they ran,
and extinguished them. The villains were next
carried to prison, amidst the deprecations of the
neighborhood.

The good Solitary, on hearing of the
fire exclaimed, "what a wonderful
of Providence, to punish guilt
more." Pausing, awhile
that Providence thought
men in their passage
with so many beings
these innocent
and these

instead of following a lawless and desperat... he would, perhaps, have perished, with all ... ily, and the villains have escaped with their ... and perplexed, he laid him down to rest ... after some time spent in gloomy reflection ... asleep.

In his dream, he fancied himself seated o... top of a high mountain, where he was accoste... a venerable figure, in long white garments, ... asked him the cause of the melancholy, expres... on his countenance.

"It is," said he, "because I am unable ... reconcile the decrees of Providence, with my id... of wisdom and justice." "That," replied t... Stranger, "is probably because thy notions ... Providence are narrow and erroneous. Th... seekest it in particular events, and dost not rais... thy survey to the great whole. Every occurrenc... in the universe is providential, because it is the ... consequence of those laws, which Divine Wisdom... has established, as most productive of the gen... good. But to select individual facts, as mo... rected by the ha... ovidence than ... because we thi... articular go... pose answered ... infallible ... error and super... me to th... ...iff." ...w.

ers escape." " And canst thou think," rejoined the Stranger, " that the single bird, made a prey of by the hawk, lies under any particular doom of Providence, or that those which fly away are more the objects of Divine favor than it ? Hawks, by nature, were made to feed upon living prey, and were endowed with strength and swiftness, to enable them to overtake and master it. Thus, life is sacrificed to the support of life. But to this destruction limits are set. The small birds are much more numerous and prolific, than the birds of prey ; and, though they cannot resist his force, they have dexterity and nimbleness of flight, sufficient, in general, to elude his pursuit. It is in this *balance*, that the wisdom of Providence is seen ; and what can be a greater proof of it, than that both species, the destroyer and his prey, have subsisted together, from their first creation. Now, look again, and tell me what thou seest."

" I see," said the Solitary, " a thick, black cloud, gathering in the sky. I hear the thunder, rolling from side to side of the vault of heaven. I behold the red lightning, darting from the bosom of darkness. Now, it has fallen on a stately tree, and shattered it to pieces, striking to the ground an ox, sheltered at its foot. Now, it falls again, in the midst of a flock of timorous sheep, and several of them are left dead, on the plain ; and see ! the shepherd himself lies extended by their side. Now, it strikes a lofty spire, and, at the same time, sets in a blaze an humble cottage, beneath. It is an awful and terrible sight !"

" It is so," returned the Stranger ; " but what dost thou conclude from it ? Dost thou not know, that, from the genial heat, which gives life to plants and animals, and ripens the fruits of the earth, proceeds this electrical fire, which, ascending to the clouds, and charging them beyond what they are able to contain, is launched, again, in burning streams, to the earth ? Must it leave its direct course to strike the tree, rather than the dome of worship, or to spend its fury on the herd, rather than the herdsman ? Millions of millions of living creatures have owed their birth to this active element ; and shall we think it strange, if a few meet their deaths from it ? Thus, the mountain torrent, that rushes down to fertilize the plain, in its course may sweep away the works of human industry, and man himself, with them ; but could its benefits be purchased, at another price ?"

" All this," said the Solitary, " I tolerably comprehend ; but, may I presume to ask, whence have proceeded the *moral evils* of the painful scenes of yesterday ? What good end is answered, by making man the scourge of man, and preserving the guilty, at the cost of the innocent ?"

" That, too," replied the venerable Stranger, " is a consequence of the same wise laws of Providence. If it was right to make man a creature of habit, and to render those things easy to him, with which he is most familiar, the sailor must, of course, be better able to shift for himself, in a shipwreck, than the passenger ; while that self-love, which is essential to the preservation of life, must, in general, cause him to consult his own safety, preferably to that of others. The same force of habit, in a way of life, full of peril and hardship, must conduce to form a rough and bold character ; sometimes, greatly to blunt the sensibility. This, under the direction of principle, will make a brave man ; without it, a robber and a murderer. In the latter case, human laws step in, to remove the evil, which they have not been able to prevent. Wickedness meets with the fate, which, sooner or later, always awaits it ; and innocence, though occasionally a sufferer, is proved, in the end, to be the surest of happiness.

"Dismiss, then, from thy mind, the care of *single events*, and rest satisfied that the *great whole* is ordered for the best. Expect not a particular interposition of Heaven, because such an interposition would seem, to thee, seasonable. Thou, perhaps, wouldst stop the vast machine of the universe, to save a fly from being crushed under its wheels. But innumerable flies and men are crushed, every day, yet the grand motion goes on, and will go on, to fulfil the benevolent intentions of its Author."

He ceased, and sleep, on a sudden, left the eyelids of the Solitary. He looked abroad from his cell, and beheld all Nature smiling around him. The rising sun shone on a clear sky. Birds were sporting in the air, and fish gliding on the surface of the waters. Fleets were pursuing their steady course, gently wafted by the pleasant breeze. Light, fleecy clouds were sailing over the blue expanse of heaven. His soul sympathized with the scene, and peace and joy filled his bosom.

THE POWER OF HABIT.

WILLIAM was, one day, reading in a book of travels, to his father, when he came to the following relation :

" The Andes, in South America, is the highest ridge of mountains in the known world.* There is a road over them, on which, about half-way between the summit and the foot, is a house of entertainment, where it is common for travellers, in their ascent and descent, to meet. The difference in their feelings, upon the same spot, is very remarkable. Those, who are descending the mountains, are melting with heat, so that they can scarcely bear any clothes upon them ; while those, who are ascending, shiver with cold, and wrap themselves up, in the warmest garments they have."

" How strange this is !" cried William. " What can be the reason of it ?"

" It is," replied his father, " a striking instance of the *power of habit* over the body. The cold

---

* This was supposed to be true, when Dr. Aikin wrote ; but it is now known that the Himmaleh Mountains, in Africa, are higher. For a map of the heights of the principal mountains in the world, see a little volume, entitled, ' Scenes in Nature, or Conversations for Children, on Land and Water,' being Vol. vii. of the *Juvenile Series* of ' THE SCHOOL LIBRARY.'

is so intense, on the tops of these mountains, that it is as much as travellers can do, to keep themselves from being frozen to death. Their bodies, therefore, become so habituated to the sensation of cold, that every diminution of it, as they descend, seems to them a degree of actual heat; and, when they are half-way down, they feel as if they were quite in a sultry climate. On the other hand, the valleys, at the foot of the mountains, are so excessively hot, that the body becomes relaxed, and sensible to the slightest degree of cold; so that, when a traveller ascends from them, towards the hills, the middle regions appear quite inclement, from their coldness."

" And does the same thing," inquired William, "always happen, in crossing high mountains?"

" It does," answered his father, "in a degree proportioned to their height, and the time taken in crossing them. Indeed, a short time is sufficient to produce similar effects. Let one boy have been playing at rolling snowballs, and another have been roasting himself before a great fire; and let them meet in the porch of the house. If you ask them how they feel, I will answer for it, you will find them as different in their accounts, as the travellers on the Andes. But this is only one example of the operations of a universal principle, belonging to human nature; for the power of habit is the same thing, whatever be the circumstance which calls it forth, whether relating to the mind or the body.

" You may consider the story you have been

reading, as a sort of simile, or parable. The central station, on the mountain, may be compared to *middle life.* With what different feelings is this regarded, by those who bask in the sunshine of opulence, and those who shrink under the cold blasts of penury !

" Suppose our wealthy neighbor were suddenly obliged to descend to our level, and live as we do ; to part with all his carriages, sell his coach-horses and hunters, quit his noble seat, with its fine park and gardens, dismiss all his train of servants, excepting two or three, and take a house like ours. What a dreadful fall would it seem to him ! how wretched would it probably make him, and how much would he be pitied by the world !

" On the other hand, suppose the laborer who lives in the next cottage, were unexpectedly to become heir to an estate, of a few hundreds a year, and, in consequence, to get around him all the comforts and conveniences that we possess ; a commodious house to inhabit, good clothes to wear, plenty of wholesome food and firing, servants, to do all the drudgery of the family, and the like. How all his acquaintance would congratulate him, and what a paradise would he seem to himself to be in ! Yet he, and our rich neighbor, and ourselves, are equally *men*, made liable, by Nature, to the same desires and necessities, and, perhaps, all equally strong in constitution, and capable of supporting hardships. Is not this fully as wonderful a difference in feeling, as that on crossing the Andes ?"

" Indeed, it is," said William.

" And the cause of it must be exactly the same, —the influence of habit."

" I think so."

" Of what importance, then, must it be, towards a happy life, to regulate our habits, so that, in the possible changes of this world, we may be more likely to be gainers than losers ?"

" But how can this be done ? Would it be right for the rich man to live like us, or for us to live like the laborer ?"

" Certainly not. But to apply the case to persons, of our middle condition : I would that we should use our advantages in such a frugal manner, as to make them essential to our happiness, as little as possible, should fortune sink us to a lower station. For, as to the chance of rising to a higher, there is no need to prepare our habits for that ; we should readily enough accommodate our feelings to such a change. To be pleased and satisfied with simple food, to accustom ourselves not to shrink from the inclemencies of the season, to avoid indolence, and take delight in some useful employment of the mind or body, to do as much as we can, for ourselves, and not expect to be waited upon, on every small occasion ; these are the habits which will make us, in some measure, independent of fortune, and secure us a moderate degree of enjoyment, under every change, short of absolute want. I will tell you a story to this purpose.

" A merchant had two sons, James and Richard.   James, from a boy, accustomed himself to every indulgence in his power, and, when he grew up, was quite a fine gentleman.   He dressed expensively, frequented public diversions, kept his hunter at a livery stable, and was a member of several convivial clubs.   At home, it was almost a footman's sole business to wait on him.   He would have thought it greatly beneath him, to buckle his own shoes ; and, if he wanted any thing at the other end of the room, he would ring the bell, and make a servant come up two flights of stairs, rather than rise from his chair, to get it. He did a little business in the counting-house, during forenoons, but devoted all his time, after dinner, to indolence and amusement.

" Richard was a very different character.   He was plain in his appearance, and domestic in his ways of life.   He gave as little trouble, as possible, and would have been ashamed to ask assistance, in doing what he could easily do for himself.   He was assiduous in business, and employed his leisure hours, chiefly, in reading, and acquiring useful knowledge.

" Both were still young and unsettled, when their father died, leaving behind him a very trifling property.   As the young men had not a capital, sufficient to follow the same line of mercantile business, in which he had been engaged, they were obliged to look out for a new plan of maintenance ; and a great reduction of expense was the first thing requisite.   This was a severe stroke to James, who found himself, at once, cut off from all the pleasures and indulgences, to which he was so habituated, that he thought life of no value without them.   He grew melancholy and deject- ed ; hazarded all of his little property in lottery tickets ; and was quite beggared.   Still, unable to think of retrieving himself, by industry and fru- gality, he accepted a commission in a newly-raised regiment, was ordered off on duty, caught a fever, and died.

"Richard, in the mean time, whose comforts were little impaired, by this change of circum- stances, preserved his cheerfulness, and found no difficulty in accommodating himself to his fortune. He engaged himself as a clerk, in a house with which his father had been connected, and lived as frugally as possible, on his salary.   It furnish- ed him with decent board, lodging, and clothing, which was all he required ; and his hours of leis- ure were nearly as many as before.   A book, or a discreet friend, always enabled him to pass an evening, pleasantly.   He gradually rose in the confidence of his employers, who increased, from time to time, his salary and emoluments.   Every in- crease was a source of gratification to him, because he was able to enjoy pleasures, which, however, habit had not made necessary to his comfort.   In process of time, he was enabled to do business for himself, and passed through life, in the enjoyment of that modest competence, which best suited his disposition."

A FRIEND IN NEED.

GEORGE CORNISH was brought up to a seafaring life. After making several voyages to the East Indies, in the capacity of mate, he obtained the command of a ship, in the country trade, there, and passed many years of his life, in sailing from one port to another, and residing, at intervals, on shore, occupied with the superintendence of commercial concerns. Having, by these means, raised a moderate fortune, and being now beyond the meridian of life, he felt a strong desire of returning to his native country, and seeing his family and friends, concerning whom, he had received no tidings, for a long time. He converted his property into money, settled his affairs, and, taking his passage for home, safely arrived there, after an absence of sixteen years.

He immediately repaired to the place of his nativity, and went to the house of an only brother, whom he had left possessed of a genteel situation in a public office. He found that his brother was dead, and the family broken up ; and he was directed to the house of one of his nieces, who was married, and settled at a small distance from town. On making himself known, he was received with great respect and affection by the married niece, and a single sister, who resided with her ; to which good reception, the idea of his bringing back with him a large fortune did not a little contribute. They pressed him, in the most urgent manner to take up his abode, there, and omitted nothing, by which they could testify their regard for so near a relation. On his part, he was sincerely glad to see them, and presented them with some valuable Indian commodities, which he had brought with him. They soon fell into conversation, concerning the family events that had taken place, during his long absence. Mutual condolences passed, on the death of their father ; their mother had been dead, long before. The Captain, in the warmth of his heart, declared his intention of befriending the survivors of the family, and his wishes of seeing the second sister as comfortably settled in the world, as the first seemed to be.

" But," said he, " are you two the only ones left ? What has become of my little, smiling playfellow, *Amelia* ? I remember her, as if it were yesterday, coming behind my chair, and giving me a sly pull, and then running away, that I might follow her, for a kiss. I shall be sorry, if any thing has happened to her."

" Alas, sir," said the eldest niece, " she has been the cause of an infinite deal of trouble to her friends ! She was always a giddy girl, and her misconduct has proved her ruin. It would be well, if we could forget her !"

" What, then," said the uncle, " has she dishonored herself ? Poor creature !"

" I cannot say," replied the niece, " that she has done so, in the worst sense of the word ; but she has disgraced herself and her family, by a hasty, foolish match with one beneath her ; and it has ended, as might have been anticipated, in poverty and wretchedness."

" I am glad," returned the Captain, " that it is no worse ; for, though I much disapprove of improper matches, yet young girls may fall into still greater evils ; and, where there is no crime, there can be no irreparable disgrace. But who was the man, and what did my brother say to it ?"

" Why, sir, I cannot say but it was partly my father's own fault ; for he took a sort of liking to the young man, who was a drawing-master, employed in the family, and would not forbid him the house, after we had informed him of the danger of an attachment between Amelia and him. So, when it was too late, he fell into a violent passion about it, which had no other effect than to drive the girl directly into her lover's arms. They married, and soon fell into difficulties. My father, of course, would do nothing for them ; and, when he died, he not only disinherited her, but made us promise no longer to look upon her as a sister."

" And you *did* make that promise ?" said the Captain, in a tone of surprise and displeasure.

" We could not disobey our parent," replied the other sister, " but we have several times sent her relief, in her necessities, though it was improper for us to see her."

" And pray, what has become of her, at last ? where is she, now ?"

" Really, she and her husband have changed their lodgings, so often, that it is some time since we heard any thing about them."

" Some time ! how long ?"

" Perhaps half a year, or more."

" Poor outcast !" cried the Captain, in a sort of muttered half-voice ; " *I* have made no promise, however, to renounce thee. Be pleased, madam," he continued, addressing himself gravely to the married niece, " to favor me with the *last* direction you had to this unfortunate sister."

She blushed, and looked confused ; and, at length, after a good deal of searching, presented it to her uncle. " But, my dear sir," said she, " you will not think of leaving us, to-day. My servant shall make all the inquiries you wish, and save you the trouble ; and, to-morrow, you can ride to town, and do as you think proper."

" My good niece," said the Captain, " I am but an indifferent sleeper ; and I am afraid things would run in my head, and keep me awake. Besides, I am naturally impatient, and love to do my business, myself. You will excuse me."

So saying, he took up his hat, and, without much ceremony, went out of the house, and took the road to town, on foot, leaving his two nieces somewhat disconcerted.

When he arrived, he went, without delay, to the place mentioned, which was in a by-street. The people, who kept the lodgings, informed him, that the persons, he inquired after, left them, several months previously, and they did not know what had become of them. This threw the Captain into great perplexity ; but, while he was considering what he should do next, the woman of the house recollected, that Mr. Bland (that was the drawing-master's name) had been employed at a certain school, where information about him might possibly be obtained. Captain Cornish hastened to the place, and was informed, by the master of the school, that such a man had, indeed, been engaged there, but had ceased to attend, for some time past.

"He was a very well-behaved, industrious young man," added the master, "but in distressed circumstances, which prevented him from making that genteel appearance which we expect in all who attend our school ; so I was obliged to dismiss him. It was a great trial to my *feelings*, I assure you, sir, to do so, but you know the thing could not be helped."

The Captain eyed him with indignant contempt, and said, " I suppose, then, sir, your *feelings* never suffered you to inquire where this poor creature lodged, or what became of him, afterwards !"

" As to that," replied the master, " every man knows his own business best, and my time is fully taken up with my own concerns ; but I believe I have a note of the lodgings he then occupied ; here it is."

The Captain took it, and, turning on his heel, withdrew, in silence. He posted away to the place, but there, also, had the mortification of learning that he was too late. The people, however, told him, that they believed he might find the family he was seeking, in a neighboring alley, at a lodging, up three flights of stairs. The Captain's heart sunk within him; however, taking a boy as a guide, he proceeded immediately to the spot. On going up the narrow, creaking staircase, he met a man coming down, with a bed on his shoulders. At the top of the landing, stood another, with a bundle of blankets and sheets. A woman, with a child in her arms, was expostulating with him, and he heard her exclaim, "Cruel! not to leave me one bed, for myself and my poor children!"

"Stop," said the Captain to the man; "set down those things." The man hesitated. The Captain renewed his command, in a peremptory tone; and then advanced towards the woman. They looked earnestly at each other. Through her pale and emaciated features, he saw something of his little smiler; and, at length, in a faint voice, he addressed her, "Are you Amelia Cornish?"

"That *was* my name," she replied.

"I am your uncle," he cried, clasping her in his arms, and sobbing, as if his heart would break.

"My uncle!" said she, and fainted.

He was just able to set her down, on the only remaining chair, and take her child from her. Two other young children came running up, and began to scream, with terror. Amelia recovered herself.

"Oh! sir, what a situation you see me in!"

"A situation, indeed!" said he. "Poor, forsaken creature! but you have *one* friend left."

He then asked what had become of her husband. She told him, that, having fatigued himself with walking, every day, to a great distance, for a little employment, which scarcely afforded them bread, he had fallen ill, and was now in a hospital; and that, after having been obliged to sell most of their little furniture and clothes, for present subsistence, their landlord had just seized their only remaining bed, for some arrears of rent. The Captain immediately discharged the debt, and, causing the bed to be brought up again, dismissed the man. He then entered into a conversation with his niece, about the events that had befallen her.

"Alas! sir," said she, "I am sensible I was greatly to blame, in disobeying my father, and leaving his roof, as I did; but, perhaps, something might be alleged in excuse; at least, years of calamity and distress may be an expiation. As to my husband, however, he has never given me the least cause of complaint; he has ever been kind and good, and what we have suffered, has been through misfortune, and not fault. To be sure, when we married, we did not consider how a family was to be maintained. His was a poor employment, and sickness, and other accidents, soon brought us to a state of poverty, from which we could never retrieve ourselves. He, poor man! was never idle, when he could help it, and denied himself every indulgence, in order

to provide for the wants of me and the children.
I did my part, too, as well as I was able.   But
my father's unrelenting severity made me quite
heart-broken ; and, though my sisters, two or
three times, gave us a little relief, in our pressing
necessities,—for nothing else could have made me
ask it, in the manner I did,—yet they would never
permit me to see them, and, for some time past,
have entirely abandoned us.   I thought Heaven
had abandoned us, too.   The hour of extreme
distress had come ; but *you* have been sent, for
our comfort."

"And your comfort, please God ! I will be,"
cried the Captain, with energy.   "You are my
own dear child, and your little ones shall be mine,
too.   Dry up your tears ; better days, I hope,
are approaching."

Evening was now coming on, and it was too
late, to think of changing lodgings.   The Captain
procured a neighbor to go out for some provisions, and other necessaries, and then took his
leave, with a promise of being with his niece,
early the next morning.   Indeed, as he proposed
going to pay a visit to her husband, she was far
from wishing to detain him longer.   He went directly from there to the hospital, and, having obtained access to the apothecary, begged to be informed of the real state of his patient, Bland.
The apothecary told him, that he labored under
a slow fever, attended with extreme dejection of
spirits, but that there were no signs of urgent
danger.

" If you will allow me to see him," said the Captain, " I believe I shall be able to administer a cordial more effectual, perhaps, than all your medicines." He was shown up to the ward, in which the poor man lay, and took a seat by his bedside. " Mr. Bland," said he, " I am a stranger to you, but I come to bring you some news of your family." The sick man roused himself, as it were, from a stupor, and fixed his eyes, in silence, on the Captain. He proceeded. " Perhaps you may have heard of an uncle, that your wife had in the East Indies ; he has come home, and—and—I am he."

Upon this, he eagerly stretched out his hand, and, taking that of Bland, which was thrust out of the bed-clothes, to meet it, gave it a cordial shake. The sick man's eyes glistened ; he grasped the Captain's hand, with all his remaining strength, and, drawing it to his mouth, kissed it with fervor. All he could say was, " God bless you ! be kind to poor Amelia !"

" I will, I will," cried the Captain ; " I will be a father to you all. Cheer up ; keep up your spirits ; all will be well !" He then, with a kind look, and another shake of the hand, wished him a good night, and left the poor man, lightened, at once, of half his disease.

The Captain went home to the coffee-house, where -he lodged, took a light supper, and went early to bed. After meditating, some time, with heartfelt satisfaction, on the work of the day, he fell into a sweet sleep, which lasted till daybreak.

The next morning, he rose early, and sallied forth, in search of furnished lodgings. After some inquiry, he met with a commodious set, in a pleasant, airy situation, for which he agreed. He then drove to Amelia, and found her and her children neat and clean, as well dressed as their poor wardrobe would admit. He embraced them, with the utmost affection, and rejoiced Amelia's heart with a favorable account of her husband. He then told them to prepare for a ride with him. The children were overjoyed at the proposal, and they accompanied him down to the coach, in high spirits. Amelia scarcely knew what to think, or expect. They drove, first, to a warehouse for ready-made linen, where the Captain made Amelia furnish herself with a complete suit of every thing necessary for present use, for the children and herself, not forgetting some shirts for her husband. Thence, they went to a clothes' shop, where the little boy was supplied with a jacket and trowsers, a hat and great coat, and the girl with another great coat and a bonnet ; both were made as happy, as happy could be. They were, next, all furnished with new shoes. In short, they had not proceeded far, before the mother and three children were all in completely new habiliments, decent, but not fine ; while the old ones were all tied up in a great bundle, and destined for some family, still poorer than they had been.

The Captain then drove to the lodgings he had taken, and which he had directed to be put in thorough order. He led Amelia up stairs, who knew not whither she was going. He brought her into a handsome parlor, and seated her in a chair. "This, my dear," said he, "is your house. I hope you will let me, now and then, come and see you, in it."

Amelia turned pale, and could not speak. At length, a flood of tears came to her relief, and she suddenly threw herself at her uncle's feet, and poured out thanks and blessings, in a broken voice. He raised her, and kindly kissing her and her children, slipped a purse of gold into her hand, and hurried down stairs.

He next went to the hospital, and found Mr. Bland, sitting up in bed, and taking some food, with apparent pleasure. He sat down by him.

"God bless you! sir," said Bland, "I see now it is all a reality, and not a dream. Your figure has been haunting me, all night, and I have scarcely been able to satisfy myself, whether I had really seen and spoken to you, or whether it was a fit of delirium. Yet my spirits have been lightened, and I have now been eating, with a relish, such as I have not experienced for many days past. But, may I ask, how is my poor Amelia, and my little ones!"

"They are well and happy, my good friend," said the Captain, "and I hope you will soon be so, along with them."

The apothecary came up, and felt his patient's pulse. "You are a lucky doctor, indeed, sir," said he, to Captain Cornish; you have cured the poor man of his fever.   His pulse is as calm as my own."

The Captain consulted him, about the safety of removing him ; and the apothecary thought that there would be no hazard in doing it, that very day.   The Captain waited the arrival of the physician, who confirmed the opinion.   A sedan chair was procured, and full directions being obtained, for his future treatment, with the physician's promise to look after him, the Captain walked before the chair, to the new lodgings.   On the knock at the door, Amelia looked out of the window, and, seeing the chair, ran down, and met her uncle and husband in the passage.   The poor man, not knowing where he was, and gazing wildly around him, was carried up stairs, and placed upon a good bed, while his wife and children assembled around it.   A glass of wine, brought by the people of the house, restored him to his recollection, when a most tender scene ensued, which the uncle closed, as soon as he could, for fear of agitating, too much, the yet feeble organs of the sick man.

By Amelia's constant attention, assisted by proper help, Mr. Bland shortly recovered ; and the whole family lost their sickly, emaciated appearance, and became healthy and happy.   The kind uncle was never long absent from them, and was always received with looks of pleasure and gratitude, that penetrated to his very heart.   He obtained for Mr. Bland a good situation, in the exercise of his profession, and took Amelia and her children into his special care. As to his other nieces, though he did not entirely break off his connexion with them, but, on the contrary, showed them occasional marks of the kindness of a relation, yet he could never look upon them, with true cordiality. And, as they had so well kept their promise, to their father, of never treating Amelia as a sister, while in her afflicted state, he took care not to tempt them to break it, now she was in a favored condition.

APHORISMS OF MIND AND MANNERS.

He, who, after a loss, immediately, without staying to lament it, sets about repairing it, has that within himself, which can control fortune.

The youth, who can sneer at exalted virtue, needs not wait for age and experience, to commence a consummate knave.

He, whose first emotion, on the view of an excellent production, is to undervalue it, will never have one of his own, to show.

The hardest trial of the heart is, whether it can bear a rival's failure, without triumph.

Him, whom, descrying at a distance, you turn out of the way to avoid, you may call your friend or benefactor, but you do not love.

The man, who, improving in skill or knowledge, improves in modesty, has an undeniable claim to greatness of mind.

18*

Bravely to contend for a good cause, is noble; silently to suffer for it, is heroical.

All professions, it is said, have their mysteries; these are precisely the points in which consists their weakness or knavery.

There are three sights most detestable; a proud priest giving his blessing, a knavish hypocrite saying his prayers, and a false patriot making an harangue.

Columbus, steering steadily westward, for a land seen only by the eye of his reason, was one of the greatest of human characters;—a projector, obstinately ruining himself, in pursuit of a visionary scheme, may be one of the foolishest, but certainly not of the lowest.

Thoroughly to try a man's patience, he must have the labor of years consumed before his eyes, in a moment; thoroughly to prove it, he must instantly begin to renew his labor.

The woman of sensibility, who preserves serenity and good temper, amid the insults of a faithless, brutal husband, wants nothing of an angel but immortality.

The woman, who rises above sickness and poverty combined, may look down upon the noisy heroism of kings and generals.

Nothing is such an obstacle to the production of *excellence*, as the power of producing what is *pretty good*, with ease and rapidity.

As reasonably expect oaks from a mushroom-bed, as great and durable products from small and hasty efforts.

Every work of great genius, and every work of great care and industry, will have its value; but mediocrity, with negligence, gives products of no value at all.

ON CHEAP PLEASURES.

THE true art of happiness consists in proportioning desires to means; or, in other words, in acquiring a relish for *procurable pleasures.*

There is scarcely a station in life, in which some attention to this point is not necessary; for desire is as much disposed to exceed the range of present enjoyment, in the highest, as in the lowest. But it is more peculiarly necessary, in those conditions, where an enlarged plan of education, and free intercourse with the superior ranks in society, have fostered lively ideas of gratifications, which fortune commonly refuses the means of obtaining.

At the head of all the pleasures, which offer themselves to the man of liberal education, may confidently be placed that derived from *books.* In variety, durability, and facility of attainment, no other can stand in competition with it; and even in intensity, it is inferior to few. Imagine, that we had it in our power to call up the shades of the greatest and wisest men, that ever existed, and oblige them to converse with us, on the most interesting topics,—what an inestimable privilege should we think it ! how superior to all common enjoyments !   But, in a well-furnished library, we, in fact, possess this power.   We can question Xenophon and Cæsar on their campaigns ; make Demosthenes and Cicero plead before us ; join in the audiences of Socrates and Plato ; and receive demonstrations from Euclid and Newton.*   In books, we have the choicest thoughts

* *Xenophon*, a celebrated general, philosopher, and historian, who was born at Athens, about four hundred and fifty years before Christ.   He was one of the many distinguished men who flourished in Athens, at that time.   He is principally famous for his retreat, with ten thousand Greeks, who were placed under his command, from the plains of Babylon, home to Greece, of which he has himself given a very interesting account.   He was also the author of other interesting works.

Caius Julius Cæsar, the first emperor of Rome, was born about one hundred years before Christ.   He was a great general, statesman, and historian, and is said to have been victorious in five hundred battles.   He wrote Commentaries on the wars in which he was engaged, on the spot where his battles were fought ; and the composition has been admired for the elegance and correctness of the style.   He was assassinated, in the Senate-house, at Rome, by several of the most eminent Senators, March fifteenth, B. C. 44, in the fifty-sixth year of his age.   See notes on pp. 59, and 156.

Demosthenes, a celebrated Athenian, whose powers of elocution were so great, that he has been deservedly called, the prince of orators, and Cicero, the greatest among the Roman orators, calls him a perfect model, and such as he himself wished to be.   He was born about three hundred and eighty-two years before Christ, and, at the early age of seventeen, he gave a proof of his eloquence and abilities, against his guardians, who had embezzled the great part of the wealth left by his father, and from whom he obtained a partial restitution of his estate.   In his youth, his talents were impeded by weak lungs, and a difficulty of pronunciation, especially of the letter r ; but he conquered all the obstacles in his way, and made of the ablest men, in their best dress. We can, at pleasure, exclude dullness and impertinence, and open our doors to wit and good sense, alone. It is needless to repeat the high commendations, that have been bestowed on the study of letters, by persons, who had free access to every other source of gratification. Instead of quoting Cicero to you, I shall, in plain terms, give

himself the greatest orator of his time. He soon became very eminent in Athens, and was placed at the head of the government. He was afterwards obliged to retire from Athens, but was recalled, for a short time, and again obliged to flee from the city, when he poisoned himself, in the sixtieth year of his age, B. C. 322.

Cicero, the most celebrated Roman orator, and also a statesman, who was born at Arpinum, (now called Arpino, and in the Kingdom of Naples,) about one hundred and three years before the commencement of the Christian era, and was killed, B. C. 43. He was, at one time, Consul, or Sovereign of Rome ; but has acquired more real fame by his writings, than by his exertions as a senator and statesman, great though those exertions were.

Socrates was the most celebrated philosopher of antiquity. He was born at Athens, where he resided, and instructed a number of illustrious pupils, by his exemplary life, as well as by his doctrines. He was falsely accused of crimes, by his enemies, and condemned to drink hemlock, (which is a deadly poison.) He died about four hundred years before the birth of our Saviour, in the seventieth year of his age.

Plato was a celebrated Greek philosopher, who resided at Athens, and was born about 429, B. C. He died on his eighty-first birthday. His name was given him, (from a Greek word, signifying *broad*,) on account of the breadth of his chest and forehead. He received an excellent education, and commenced his literary career, by writing poems and tragedies. At the age of twenty, he was introduced to Socrates, and continued to be one of his pupils, for eight years. After the death of Socrates, he travelled over Greece, you the result of my own experience, on this subject. If domestic enjoyments have contributed, in the first degree, to the happiness of my life, (and I should be ungrateful, not to acknowledge that they have,) the pleasures of reading have, beyond all question, held the second place. Without books, I have never been able to pass a single day, to my entire satisfaction ; with them, no day

Sicily, and Egypt, and then retired to the groves of Academus, about an eighth of a mile from the city of Athens, where he resided, and gave his instructions, for forty years. His lectures were attended by a crowd of learned, noble, and illustrious, pupils, and his fame continued to increase, and his school to become more frequented, till the close of his life. His works are numerous, and have been the admiration of every age and country.

Euclid, a celebrated mathematician, who was born in Alexandria, in Egypt, about two hundred and eighty years before Christ. He distinguished himself by his writings, on music and geometry. The most celebrated of his works, is his ' Elements of Geometry,' which is in use, at the present day. He established a school at Alexandria, which became so famous, that, from his time to the conquest of Alexandria, by the Saracens, (A. D. 646,) no mathematician was found, who had not studied at Alexandria. Ptolemy, King of Egypt, was one of his pupils ; and it was in answer to a question of this King, whether there was not a shorter way of coming at Geometry, than by his Elements, that Euclid made the celebrated answer, that " there is no royal way, or path, to Geometry."

Sir Isaac Newton, one of the greatest mathematicians and philosophers, the world has produced, was born in Woolstrop, in England, on Christmas day, A. D. 1642, and died, twentieth of March 1727, in the eighty-fifth year of his age. An extended notice of him may be found in the first volume of the ' Pursuit of Knowledge under Difficulties,' forming one of the volumes of the larger series of ' THE SCHOOL LIBRARY.'

has been so dark, as not to have its pleasure. Even pain and sickness have, for a time, been charmed away, by them. By the easy provision of a book in my pocket, I have frequently worn through long nights and days, in the most disagreeable parts of my profession, with all the difference in my feelings, between calm content and fretful impatience. Such occurrences have afforded me full proof, both of the possibility of being cheaply pleased, and of the consequence it is, to the sum of human felicity, not to neglect minute attentions, to make the most of life, as it passes.

Reading may, in every sense, be called a *cheap* amusement. A *taste for books*, indeed, may be made expensive enough ; but that is a taste for editions, bindings, paper, and type. If you are satisfied with getting at the sense of an author, in some commodious way, a crown,* at a stall, will supply your wants, as well as a guinea,† at a shop.‡ Learn, too, to distinguish between books to be *perused*, and books to be *possessed*. Of the former, you may find an ample store, in every subscription library, the proper use of which, to a scholar, is to furnish his mind, without loading his shelves. No apparatus, no appointment of time and place, is necessary for the enjoyment of read-

* A crown is about one dollar and fifteen cents.

† A guinea is about five dollars and seven cents.

‡ In Europe, book stalls are more common than in this Country, though we have a few of them, here. At these stalls, old books are sold much cheaper, than new ones can be procured at the bookstores.

ing.   From the midst of bustle and business,
you may, in an instant, by the magic of a book,
plunge into scenes of remote ages and countries,
and disengage yourself from present care and fatigue.   "Sweet pliability of man's spirit, (cries
Sterne, on relating an occurrence of this kind,)
that can at once surrender itself to illusions,
which cheat expectation and sorrow of their
weary moments!"

The next of the procurable pleasures, that I
shall point out to you, is that of *conversation.*
This is a pleasure of higher zest, than that of
reading ; since, in conversing, we not only receive
the sentiments of others, but impart our own ; and,
from this reciprocation, a spirit and interest arise,
which books cannot give, in an equal degree.
Fitness for conversation must depend upon the
store of ideas laid up in the mind, and the faculty
of communicating them.   These, in a great degree, are the results of education, and the habit
of society ; and, to a certain point, they are favored by superiority of condition.   But this is
only to a certain point ; for, when you arrive at
that class, in which sensuality, indolence, and dissipation, are fostered by excess of opulence, you
lose more, by diminished energy of mind, than you
gain, by superior refinement of manner and elegance of expression.

I would not, however, inculcate too fastidious a
taste, with respect to the subject and style of conversation, provided it possess the essentials of
sound sense and useful knowledge.   Among those,

who have enjoyed little of the benefit of education, you will often find persons of natural sagacity, and a turn for remark, who are capable of affording both entertainment and instruction. Who would not wish to have been acquainted with Franklin, when a journeyman printer, even though he had never risen to be one of the most distinguished characters of the age ? Information, indeed, may be procured from almost any man, in affairs belonging to his particular way of life ; and, when we fall into company, from which little is to be expected, with regard to general topics, it is best to give the conversation a turn towards the technical matters, with which they may be acquainted, whence some profit may be made out of the most unpromising materials. *Man*, too, in every condition, is a subject, well worthy of examination ; and the speculatist may derive much entertainment, from observing the manners and sentiments of all the various classes of mankind, in their several occupations and amusements.

Another source of cheap pleasure is the *study of Nature*. So many advantages, with respect to health, tranquillity of mind, useful knowledge, and inexhaustible amusement, are united in this study, that I should not fail most warmly to recommend it to your notice, had you not already acquired a decided taste for its pursuits. Here, again, I can speak from my own experience ; for the study of English botany caused several Summers to glide away with me, in more pure and active delight, than almost any other single object

19 **VIII.**

ever afforded me. It rendered every ride and
walk interesting, and converted the plodding
rounds of business into excursions of pleasure.
From the impression of these feelings, I have ever
regarded, as perfectly superfluous, the pains taken
by some of the friends of natural history, to show
its utility, in reference to the common purposes
of life. Many of their observations, indeed, are
true, and may serve to gain patrons for the study,
among those who measure every thing by the
standard of economical value ; but is it not enough
to open a source of copious and cheap amusement, which tends to harmonize the mind, and
elevate it to worthy conceptions of Nature and its
Author ? If I offer a man happiness, at an easy
rate, unalloyed by any debasing mixture, can I
confer on him a greater blessing ? Nothing is
more favorable to enjoyment, than the combination of bodily exertion and ardor of mind. This,
the researches of natural history afford, in great
perfection ; and, such is the immense variety of
its objects, that the labors of the longest life cannot exhaust them.

The study of Nature is, in itself, a cheap study ;
yet it may be pursued, in a very expensive manner, by all the apparatus of cabinets, purchased
collections, prints, and drawings. But, if you will
content yourself with the great Book of Nature,
and a few of its ablest expositors, together with
the riches your own industry may accumulate, you
will find enough of it, within your compass, to
answer all reasonable purposes of instruction and

amusement. We are both acquainted with an
excellent Naturalist, who, by a proper application
of the time and money he has been able to spare,
out of a common writing school, has made himself the possessor of more curious and accurate
knowledge, than falls to the lot of many owners
of the most costly treasures. The recollection
of his modest merit, and scientific content, will
ever, I am sure, endear to you these fertile stores
of cheap delight.

A taste for the sublime and beautiful of Nature,
as exhibited in her larger works, and resulting
from the varied combinations of her external forms,
is also productive of many exquisite pleasures,
which few persons are, at all times, precluded
from enjoying. To feel these, in a supreme degree, a mind, enriched by literature, and expand-
ed by fancy and reflection, is necessary ; and, in
particular, a high relish for poetry is almost an
essential accompaniment. Much pains do not
seem requisite, in cultivating this species of enjoyment ; for it obtrudes itself, unsought, upon every elegant mind, and the danger is, lest the desire should too soon exhaust its objects. More
uneasy longings, after what lay beyond my reach,
have preyed upon my imagination, on reading de-
scriptions of the striking scenes of Nature, visited
by travellers, than on reflecting on all the other
advantages, which fortune and leisure have to
bestow. Yet, certainly, I would not wish to have
been less sensible, than I am, to this source of
pleasurable emotions. They may be rendered

more distinct and varied, by calling in a taste for what is properly termed the *picturesque*, or a reference of the natural scene, to its imitations and improvements by the pencil. But this, I conceive to be almost necessarily connected with practical skill, in the art of painting ; and, unless it were made subservient to the purposes of this art, I should apprehend, that more might be lost, by opening an inlet to fastidious nicety, than would be gained, by viewing things with a more learned eye.

This remark would naturally lead me to consider the pleasures to be derived from the practice of ornamental arts, and from the contemplation of their productions in others. But, though I am fully sensible of the pleasing addition these make to the general stock of human enjoyment, yet, with respect to most individuals, they scarcely come within the catalogue of cheap pleasures. A taste for them must be formed, early in life, must be cultivated with much assiduity, and at considerable expense, both of time and money. They are not of all times and places, but require apparatus and opportunity. They are with difficulty kept within bounds, and are continually disposed to desert the easy and simple, in pursuit of what is more complex and elaborate. A taste for music appears to me, as far as I can judge from observation, alone, to be eminently of this kind. Where it is marked out by Nature, as in some cases it manifestly is, and can be cultivated early and advantageously, it is capable, I doubt not, of affording the most exquisite delights; but then, it will probably take place of all other ornamental acquirements. And, though such a sacrifice may be worth making, under the circumstances described, yet to make it, with a view of *creating* a taste for any pursuit, merely amusive, is, I think, to estimate, falsely, the value of things. If, however, experience shows, that musical pleasures may be enjoyed in moderation, and so as to make an agreeable variety, without occupying the place of any thing preferable, my objections are at an end. The same may be said of drawing, and various other tastes and acquisitions, concerning which, accident and inclination, if regulated by prudence, may be suffered to determine the choice.

I have now, I think, pointed out to you, sources, which will supply sufficient *materials*, of easily procurable pleasure, if you bring to them, what is absolutely essential to the success of any external means of happiness,—a mind, in harmony with itself. This, nothing but conscious worth and virtue can bestow.

HISTORY AND BIOGRAPHY ESTIMATED.

THAT, to a human being, no study can be more important, than that of the character and fortune of mankind, may be almost assumed, as a self-evident proposition. What, indeed, can be so necessary, to all ranks and conditions, as a knowledge of the creatures with whom they are to live and act, on whom so large a share of their happiness is to depend, and from whose fate they are enabled to infer their own?

History and biography are the great records of man; the first, of what he has been and done, collectively, the second, of the same, individually. The limits between the two cannot exactly be defined; for, on the one hand, societies being composed of individuals, the history of the former consists of the actions of the latter; and, on the other, the actions of individuals being frequently displayed in their effects on societies, they cannot be considered, without entering into the discussions of history. This intercommunication of subject, however, admirably fits them for throwing light upon one another, and supplying each other's deficiencies. History, as it has been too much the custom to compose it, gives a distinct view only of those *great* events, as they are called, which, from their uniformity and simplicity, instruct less, in the real nature of mankind, than the story of domestic and civil life. Wars, confederacies, treaties, contentions for supreme power, and the final triumph of the strong over the weak, fill, with few exceptions, the whole space of the historical tablet; and the individuals who are brought forward on its canvass, and supply it with figures of portraiture, are often less distinguished from each other, by characteristic marks, than many who remain unnoticed in the crowd.

Biography has taken the personages of history, and, by painting them as single portraits, has given more exact delineations of their features ; but it has likewise selected many from the groups of common life, and has thereby made a display of human character, vastly more copious, varied, and distinct, than is to be found in history, alone.

If, on this comparison, the advantage seems to lie on the side of biography, it must, however, be confessed, that this is liable to peculiar causes of misrepresentation, which, if not corrected, either by general history, or by the spirit of philosophy, are extremely apt to mislead. Almost every professed biographer sits down with the intention of making a *hero* of his subject ; and not only raises his personal character above its merits, but gives him an undue share of consequence, in the public events in which he was concerned, or in the advancement of the art or science in which he was eminent. Some, in their gross daubings, lay on every glaring color of moral and intellectual excellence, to decorate their portrait, without the least attention to nature and congruity. Others, more artful, and therefore more delusive, only exaggerate qualities really possessed, palliate or wholly conceal defects, and form such a general resemblance, as a flattering painter gives to draughts, which are designed rather to please than to strike.

In biographical writing, almost every thing tends to nourish this fault of favoritism. The original choice of subject is usually made from some cir-

cumstance of predilection ; such as personal friendship, community of studies, of profession, of party,
or country. It is frequently to be lamented, that
the very connexion, which affords the means of
accurate information concerning a person, gives a
bias to the mind of the writer, and unfits him for
faithful narration. Such a relation as that of
master, patron, or benefactor, while it brings the
superior within the eye of the inferior, can scarcely
fail of imposing upon the latter the shackles of
gratitude or enthusiastic admiration, and thereby
incapacitating him for the exercise of that critical
scrutiny, which alone can develope the secret
springs and motives of action, and bring to view
the latent discriminations of character. Even the
simple propensity, of rendering a picture the perfect exemplar of its genus, seduces an ingenious
writer to heighten his touches and improve effect,
at the expense of reality.

With respect to the grosser inducements to
violate truth, which operate upon biographers, historians, and the eulogists,* of every species, who
receive pay for their labors, it is scarcely necessary
to bestow particular animadversion upon them,
since, whenever they are detected, they will be
held in due contempt ; and it is not often, that
they can escape detection. In some, indeed,
the temptation, or rather obligation, to partiality,
has been so unblushingly displayed, that it is wonderful they could ever have been thought capable

* Those who eulogize, or write eulogies, or encomiums
upon others.

of effecting their purpose. What reader of common sagacity would look for a faithful account of transactions in the pages of a royal or national historiographer ?* The office has now, I believe, by the good sense of modern times, been reduced to a sinecure ; but when Louis XIV.† made his unjust and ostentatious expedition into the Low Countries,‡ he actually took with him the two greatest writers in his kingdom, Boileau§ and Racine,‖ (poets, both, and therefore well practised in fiction,) in order to record the great actions he was to perform, by means of his generals. The best proof they gave of their judgement, on the occasion, was, that they never published a single sentence of what they composed in their new capacity. This instance of vanity and absurdity may be added to the examples of the benefits proceeding from the boasted alliance between the learned and the great.

* Formerly, kings had in their service persons, who were employed to write the histories and recount the deeds of their masters.

† See note on page 156, for an account of Louis XIV.

‡ The kingdom of the Netherlands is called the Low Countries, from being situated on a very low level. Holland, Belgium, Flanders, and other provinces, are included in the term.

§ *Despréaux Nicholas Boileau*, a celebrated French poet, was born near Paris, A. D. 1636, and died in 1711. Some of his works met with extraordinary applause.

‖ *Jean Racine*, a celebrated French tragic poet, was born December 21, 1639, at Ferte Milon, a town in France, about sixty miles from Paris. He spent most of his life at Paris, devoted entirely to poetry. He died April 22, 1699.

The more distinct the limits of history and biography are kept, the more likely, I conceive, will each be to be written with purity, and to prove an effectual check upon the other. I cannot, therefore, approve the method of writing select portions of history, marked as the *age* of this or that distinguished person. Such an association gives, indeed, a peculiar interest to the work, and aids the memory, in referring facts to their proper era ; but it can scarcely fail of impressing the reader with exaggerated ideas of the consequence of the individual, from whom the denomination is taken. I have often been struck with the silent and unobserved manner, in which some of these great personages steal out of the world, in the narration of a general history, leaving the political machine to go its usual round, without feeling the change of a nominal director ; whereas the reader, who comes to the conclusion of his *age* with its hero, would be apt to suppose, that the whole form of the world must be altered, and a new order of things commence, with the date of a new period. Neither, in the plan of one of these works, can the writer easily avoid incongruity and disproportion. He will think himself obliged to enter, with minuteness, into every particular which relates personally to his hero, while he passes over, with little notice, the most important events of the age, which have not such a connexion. Thus, the views he affords of the period will be at once defective and redundant, indistinct and minute.

The partiality which has associated the name of Pope Leo X.* with the most flourishing era of Italian† arts and literature, has still less foundation. His pontificate, of less than nine years, was distinguished, indeed, by the munificent patronage of the fine arts, and of polite learning; but the talents, which his love for show and splendor led him to employ, had already arrived at fame and maturity, and had been objects of the admiration of several of his predecessors, as well as of the public, in general. Though he had the credit of patronising Vida,‡ yet his own taste in literature was degraded by a love of burlesque and low buffoonery, which is allowed to have been injurious to the cause of learning, as much as it was derogatory from the dignity of his station. He had probably a purer taste in the arts of design; but the pencil of Raphael§ was inspired by genius,

* *Leo X.*, whose name was Giovanni de Medici, was born at Florence, in Tuscany, A. D. 1475. He received a good education, and, after being employed in several offices, was elected Pope, in 1513, in the thirty-eighth year of his age. He then assumed the title of Leo X. He died December 1, 1521.

† Belonging to Italy.

‡ *Mark Jerome Vida* was a celebrated Latin poet, born A. D. 1490, of poor parents, but of noble descent. He received a good education, and was made Bishop of Alba, in 1532. He died September 27, 1566. He was the author of many poetical works.

§ *Raphael*, or *Raffaelo*, the greatest painter of the modern, or last of the ancient, school of art, was born on Good Friday, March 8, 1483, and died at Rome, on Good Friday, April 7, 1520. His paintings are very celebrated.

working after specimens of consummate excellence, and not by the influence of "Leo's golden days," which did not commence, till painting was brought to its highest perfection. The merit of a real proficient, in any one of the nobler departments of human skill, is, in my opinion, so much superior to that of a mere patron, especially of one who can bestow honors and rewards at the public expence, that I cannot but think it unworthy of e foi, to be put in the train and made subservient to the glory of the latter.

From the preceding remarks, I would deduce the general inference, that, in order to obtain a just view, either of the series of cause and effect on which the great political changes of mankind have depended, or of the progressive state of arts and sciences, we should take, as guides, those writers, who have treated these topics historically, without any further notice of individuals, than their share in the matter has strictly demanded ; but that to acquire a knowledge of what man intrinsically is, of what he is capable of effecting, of all the variations of his character, and the causes which concur in forming them, the narrations of biography must be consulted. On these, alone, in conjunction with our observations of the passing scenery of life, can we depend for the rectifying of those false ideas, which the theories of speculatists,* and the fictions of poets and novelists, are continually obtruding upon our minds,

---

* Those who speculate, schemers.

and the combined mass of which probably constitutes a much larger portion of our opinion, than we suspect. Every one, even moderately conversant with works of inven.on, must frequently, I doubt not, when searchin for examples to corroborate moral or metap! , .ical theories, have found himself recurring, unawares, to the characters and events containe' in such works, in preference to those of real fe. But I have already taken occasion to remark, that no .er, h w great soever be his skill and usual huwny in copying Nature, deserves to be quoted as authority, in his fancy-pieces, especially in those which aim at giving pleasure and surprise by means of novelty. More delusive than these, however, are the writers, who, in order to support a philosophical system, weave a tissue of fictitious characters and adventures, expressly calculated for presenting such a view of human nature as may suit their prior reasonings, and derived entirely from speculation, uncorrected by experience. In such pretended histories, it may easily happen, that the whole representation of mankind is as void of truth, as if it had been made for the supposed inhabitants of Saturn or Sirius ;* and a reasonable preposses-

---

* Our young readers are undoubtedly familiar with the names of the different primary planets, which are seen in the heavens, of which Saturn is one of the largest and most distant. They are also probably aware, that the ancient astronomers arranged the stars into groups, or clusters, which are called constellations. To these constellations they assigned names, according to their fancy, or from the appearance which they imagined the stars presented to the eye. The twelve

sion will lie against systems, which dare not trust their proof to appeals to the world, as it is, but must invent a world of their own, for the display and confirmation of their principles.

Biography, sufficiently minute, and composed with judgement, is the best corrective of these fanciful pictures of human nature, particularly, by the insight it affords into the circumstances which, from early youth, have contributed to the formation of character, moral and intellectual. It will give the true discrimination, between the effects of original constitution and those of association, in forming the peculiar bent of the mind ; the theoretical discussion of which may be carried on, for ever, by the aid of gratuitous suppositions, without coming to a decision. Genuine biography will exhibit, on the one hand, such manifest instances of irresistible propensities to certain pursuits, and of settled casts of temper, appearing from the first dawnings of reason, as must convince any, but a determined theorist, that there are primary and radical differences in minds, which give the leading color to character, and are capable only of being modified, not changed. On the

signs, or constellations, of the Zodiac,—the Ram, the Bull, the Twins, &c., are familiar to our readers ; and so, probably, are some of the other constellations, as the Great Bear, and others. Sirius, (called also the Dog star,) is a very bright star, of the largest size ; the brightest, indeed, to be seen in our firmament. It is called the Dog star, because it is situated in that constellation, or cluster of stars, which the ancients called the Little Dog. Some others of these constellations are mentioned in a note to page 65.

other hand, it will distinctly show, that early impressions often exert an influence, through all the subsequent periods of life ; and that principles and opinions are usually the result of such associations, as are capable of direction, and consequently leave ample scope for plans of education, and other processes of instruction and melioration.

From biography may also be learned the fallacy of those analogical conclusions, respecting the attributes of the mind, which suppose a necessary coexistence between certain moral and intellectual qualities, according to some hypothetical notions of their constitutional cause. This is a copious source of misrepresentation, in the modern philosophical works of fiction, and one, in my opinion, capable of doing much mischief. By confounding the active and passive qualities of mind, they have made the degree, in which impressions are received, a test of the energies ready to be exerted. Thus, passion, to the verge of madness, sensibility, so exquisite as to become disease, and uncontrollable ardor of desire, are painted as the constant concomitants of high intellectual powers, vigor of imagination, and all the nobler virtues of the heart. Hence, youth are taught to regard, as symptoms of an exalted soul, actions and propensities, the most injurious to society and the individual ; and to look with scorn upon that sedateness and moderation of character, which the most judicious moralists have accounted the perfection of humanity. But biography not only presents combinations of qualities, which baffle *all* speculative reasonings concerning the mental constitution, but, in particular, it contradicts the false analogies, above hinted at. In the enumeration of great writers, admirable inventors, active philanthropists, consummate generals, profound politicians,—of all those *master-minds*, in short, who lead the opinions and direct the fate of mankind, I am convinced a majority will be found, whose calm and unruffled tempers allowed an uninterrupted exercise to their intellectual faculties ; who were men of method, order, and regularity, in full possession of themselves, and capable of directing, at will, the whole force of their minds, upon the objects in which they were engaged. On the other hand, characters of violence, caprice, and uncontrolled desire, so properly termed by the Romans *impotentia animi*,* are most frequently to be met with among the degenerate possessors of hereditary power, or the unworthy favorites of fortune, raised, by some frivolous accomplishments, to stations, for which Nature never designed them. Or, if they are found in alliance with genius and elevated sentiment, that genius is usually wasted on unequal and abortive efforts, and that sentiment leads to nothing but vain resolutions and unavailing regrets.

Those characters in biography are most instructive and animating, in which we see persevering efforts overcoming a crowd of obstacles, and distinguished eminence gradually rising out

---

* Outrageous ; ungovernable.

of moderate beginnings. This is, in fact, the discipline through which some of the greatest names among mankind have passed ; and it may be asserted, that none of the original favorites of Nature and fortune have attained a superiority, so solid and durable, as that acquired by such a course of probation. But it is not from volatile, impetuous characters, however active and ardent, that such a steady career in proficiency is to be expected ; and that kind of rapid, restless genius, which is fired by every splendid prospect, and obtains easy conquests in every new field of exertion, is rather an impediment than a help, in the progress to excellence.

The only proper object of history and biography, beyond that of mere amusement, is *the study of man*. The application of this study belongs to philosophy, which is, faithfully, impartially, and upon an extensive scale, to make use of the materials thus provided. To direct that we should sit down to the perusal of historical narratives, with the purpose of finding in them the confirmation of certain moral or religious principles, previously adopted, is to invert the order of rational deduction, and make the conclusion precede the premises. Amid the immense collection of facts, recorded in general and particular histories, examples may be found, to confirm almost any supposition, relative to the chain of cause and effect, and the direction of human affairs, that the reader chooses to assume ; but what is acquired by this partial mode of selection, except a reenforcement

20*

to prejudice, and a stock of weak and superstitious judgements ?   Some of the lessons, deducible from the knowledge of mankind, are tolerably obvious ; but many more are involved in a thick mist of doubt, which can be cleared away only by calm and laborious investigation.

ON THE BEST MODE OF ENCOUNTER-ING THE EVILS OF LIFE.

It is scarcely necessary to make the formal observation, that no one can pass through life, without having a certain share of evil to sustain. The most fortunate man is sufficiently sensible of this truth ; and, how unmixed soever his present enjoyments may be, he cannot, at all times, banish from his reflection, the uncertain tenure by which he holds them, and his inability to ward off the strokes of calamity, to which he is continually exposed.   The proper conduct under misfortune must, then, be a topic, interesting to every thinking being.   I have found it so, to myself, and have made it the frequent subject of my thoughts.   If any thing valuable has been the result of these meditations, I cannot but desire that you should participate in it.

Two moral duties, different and apparently opposite in their natures, occur to the mind, on the prospect of the evils of life ;—resignation under them, and resistance to them.   Natural temper will perhaps give such a decided bias to one or the other of these modes of conduct, that no precept will influence persons of very different characters, to act alike on these occasions ; yet, since, in all moral cases, there is a real ground for preferring one determination to another, it is incumbent on a creature of reason to make his preference rightly, and not passively to follow mere propensities. Besides, it will probably be found, on inquiry, that there is not such an opposition, between the two duties abovementioned, as at first sight may appear ; and that each may properly take its turn, according to circumstances. These I shall proceed to consider.

One class of misfortunes, to which we are liable, may be stated to be, the loss or deprivation of valuable things, which we once possessed, and which are capable of being restored. It cannot be doubted, that, in these cases, the dictate of Nature is, to repair the loss, in the best manner we are able ; and the more speedily and decisively the task is undertaken, the more certain is the indication of strength and vigor of mind. A savage, returning to his hut, finds it burned to the ground. If he is of a lazy or desponding disposition, he will perhaps say, " Well then, I will creep among the thickest bushes I can find, and trouble myself no more with building." This may be termed resignation ; nay, some would perhaps dignify it with the name of philosophy : in fact, however, it is apathy and imbecility. The stronger-souled savage will instantly take his hatch-

et, and repair to the forest, in order to select materials for a new hut.   This spirit may be traced
through every condition of life, and every where
is the object of just admiration.   Horace* plays
the stoic too much, when he says, disparagingly,
of the tempest-tossed merchant,

> " Untaught a scanty lot to bear,
>   See him his shattered bark repair :"

for, whatever system of happiness a man has adopted, he is right to pursue it with vigor, his notions
remaining the same.   Though the philosopher
may prove, that the possession of a crown is rather
a burden than a blessing, we cannot help admiring
the deposed prince, who bravely exerts himself,
for the recovery of what he thinks his birthright.
Horace was sufficiently sensible of the merit of
bearing up against misfortunes, in the person of
Homer's Ulysses,† whom he characterizes, in true
poetical language, as

> "Still buoyant, ' mid the waves of adverse fate."

The hero was not less the *patient*, the *much-en-*
during man, on account of this struggle.   He did
not complain, but he acted.   In like manner, it
is the generous injunction of the Sibyl to Æneas,‡

> " Yield not to ills, but push a bolder course
>   Where Fortune points the way."

* *Horace* was one of the ancient poets, who died about
eight years before the birth of our Saviour.

† See note on page 64.

‡ The *Sibyl* was an ancient prophetess and priestess of
Apollo.   There were ten celebrated ones, as at Delphi, Cu-

Among the real characters of antiquity, Aristomenes,* the Messenian chief, seems to have been peculiarly distinguished by this buoyancy of spirit, this *renitency*† of the mind, against the pressure of adversity. Wounded, defeated, thrown into a dungeon, he still preserved his hopes and exertions ; and, when the foes of his country thought him at the last extremity, they suddenly found him more formidable than ever. The Scottish hero, Wallace,‡ seems closely to have resembled him,

---

mæ, &c. The one at Cumæ is said to have come to the palace of the Roman Emperor, Tarquin the Second, and shown him nine books, containing prophecies, demanding three hundred pieces of gold for them, which Tarquin refused to give. She then burnt three of them in his presence, and demanded the same sum for the remaining six, which he still refused. She then threw three more into the fire, demanding the same sum for the remaining three, which the king, astonished at her behavior, is said to have given, when the Sibyl disappeared and was never afterwards seen. These three books were afterwards preserved as sacred, and were called the Sibylline leaves, or verses. These priestesses were consulted as oracles, and were supposed to be able to foretell future events. It was the one at Cumæ, who was consulted by Æneas. *Æneas* was a Trojan prince, whose adventures are celebrated by the poet Virgil, in his poem called the Æneid. He is supposed to have flourished at the time of the Trojan War, about one thousand one hundred and eighty-four years before the Christian era.

* *Aristomenes* was a famous general of Messenia, a large country in Greece. He acquired the surname of *Just* from his equity, to which he joined the true valor, perseverance, and sagacity, of a general. He was killed about six hundred and seventy-one years before Christ.

† Elasticity, resistance to pressure.

‡ *Sir William Wallace* was a celebrated Scottish patriot

in this respect.   Such a disposition of mind is
shown in small things, as well as in great.   It is
mentioned, as a characteristic trait of Charles
XII.,* of Sweden, that once, after he had sat up
all night, to dictate despatches, his secretary, when
they were finished, having thrown ink, instead of
sand, over the writing, the King very coolly said,
" then we must begin again ;" and went on, as if
nothing had happened.   This was worthy of
Charles, at Bender.†   I have read of a scholar,
who, in a somewhat similar case, had an opportunity of displaying as much heroism, as any king
or general, in their greatest actions ; for the emer-
gency was as great to him, as a contest for a kingdom to them.   An accidental fire had destroyed
his papers prepared for publication, the labor of
many years.   He recommenced the work that
very day.‡   The Romans made it criminal, to

and hero who performed many valiant deeds, in his efforts to
liberate his country from its subjugation to England, about
A. D. 1800.   He was appointed Regent of Scotland, and
gained several victories ; but, owing to the intrigues of some
of the Scottish lords, who were jealous of his power, he resigned the regency, and was afterwards betrayed into the
hands of the English, by whom he was put to death, August,
23, 1805.

    * For a notice of this King, see note on pages 151, 152.

    † *Bender* is the chief city of a district in Turkey, where
Charles XII. found an asylum after his reverses, and resided
for some time.   •

    ‡ Sir Isaac Newton one morning shut up his little dog in his
room, and, on returning, found that the animal, by upsetting
a candle on his desk, had destroyed the labors of several years.
On perceiving his loss, he only exclaimed, " O Diamond !

despair of the Commonwealth; and, after the greatest disasters, their only thought was, how to repair them. This was the spirit that rendered them invincible. Horace well understood this distinguishing character of his countrymen, where he introduces Hannibal* as lamenting his decline of fortune, against so pertinacious a foe.

" Like the firm ilex, shorn with axe severe,
  That blackens on the mountain's wood-crowned side,
  'Mid wounds and death their dauntless fronts they rear,
  And gain, from steel itself, new force and pride.''

Hitherto, there seems no doubt of the part a manly mind will act, under loss or misfortune. But it is a more difficult point, to decide how far attempts ought to be made, to redress those original wrongs (if so they may be termed) of fortune, whereby privations are incurred, of advantages highly esteemed by the world. Such are mean birth, indigence, and natural defects, which doom a man, without extraordinary exertions, to pass a whole life in poverty and obscurity. The difficulty, here, arises from the want of agreement respecting real goods ; for, while the worldly man, without hesitation, fixes his desires upon wealth, rank, and splendor, as almost the only objects

Diamond ! you little know the mischief you have done.''
The grief occasioned by this loss, however, seriously injured his health.

* *Hannibal*, or *Annibal*, was a celebrated General of Carthage, who was born about two hundred and fifty years before Christ. He was victorious in many battles with the Romans, but at last was defeated, and, being deserted by his own countrymen, killed himself by poison, B. C. 183.

worthy of pursuit, the philosopher affects to regard them rather as impediments towards the attainment of those mental excellencies, which, alone, in his estimation, possess genuine value.   Here, then, commences the contest between ambition and content, concerning which, so many fine things have been said, in verse and prose.   It is not my intention to collect them, for your perusal, since oratorical effusions, on general topics, are of little use in the decision of particular points of conduct ; and much must be left, in this case, to individual feeling.   I do not greatly esteem those efforts for the attainment of riches, alone, which are made by persons, who might, by a proper improvement of the faculties bestowed upon them, acquire a moderate share of respect and comfort in an humble station.   Yet I cannot withhold my admiration from the man of superior talents, who struggles through all the obstacles that fortune has thrown in his way, with the noble ambition of raising himself to that distinction, in science or letters, which may place him on his proper level in society. Though he may partly concur with the vulgar, in the final objects of his wishes, (who, indeed, can pretend not to partake in the common sentiments of mankind ?) yet the mode of pursuit throws an adventitious dignity over the acquisition.   The unmeaning title of modern knighthood could add nothing to the illustrious name of NEWTON,* yet

* For a notice of Sir Isaac Newton, see note on page 288, and also the first volume of the ' Pursuit of Knowledge under Difficulties,' forming one of the volumes of the larger Series

it was honorable to have attained it, by means of eminence like his, and the title gained a consequence, by his thinking it worthy his acceptance. Biography affords many animating examples, of the force of genius and vigor united, to elevate a man to the celebrity, for which Nature had marked him out, though fortune had refused to concur in the destination. Of these, I recollect none, more worthy of being admired, than that of Linnæus ;* who, though so indigent, at the university, as to be obliged to patch his own shoes, persisted, amid scorn and hardships of every kind, in the steady pursuit of that course of study, which he knew to be essential to the great objects he had in view, and which, aided by the confident presage of future fame and distinction, bore up his spirits, against every discouragement.

To rise to eminence, in his own profession, cannot but be esteemed a fair and laudable mark of ambition, to every man, how humble soever the stage, from which he makes his commencement ; for profession is a common character, to all the individuals belonging to it, and forms a reasonable ground for equal expectations. Through the influence of this ambition, it has happened,

of 'The School Library.' He was made a knight by Queen Anne, in the year 1705.

* For an account of this celebrated Botanist, see a volume entitled ' Social Evenings, or Historical Tales for Youth, by Miss Mary E. Lee,' being the fifth volume of the *Juvenile Series* of ' The School Library ;' and also the first volume of the ' Pursuit of Knowledge under Difficulties,' referred to in the note on page 240.

that the most eminent, in every walk, have usually been those, who have labored under the greatest disadvantages in their origin. Such men must, of necessity, be endowed with superior genius and force of mind, as well as with particular talents for their profession, in order to arrive at distinction in it ; whereas one, for whom a way of life is chosen, merely on account of circumstances of convenience or expected advantage, may attain a certain degree of success, with moderate talents and small exertions.   The lives of painters, whose art, perhaps beyond any other, affords fair proof of the relative merit of its professors, abound in instances of this fact.   Boys, employed to grind colors, have often turned out celebrated artists, while favored pupils of the greatest schools have never been heard of.

To conclude the head of *Content ;* I must confess, that I doubt whether this principle ever enabled a person permanently to rest satisfied, in a state of degradation and obscurity, who was conscious of powers to raise him to honor and reputation.   Such a one must have frequent misgivings, concerning the motives of his quietism ; and must suspect indolence and timidity, where an indulgent observer might perhaps give him credit for a generous contempt of the objects of vulgar admiration.   The philosopher and the cœnobite* may indeed, without regret, have resigned the pursuit of riches and grandeur, but they will not readily

* One of a religious order, living in a convent or a community.

become insensible to the charms of glory and influence. Diogenes* in his tub, and Simeon† on his pillar, were as unwilling to remain undistinguished in the throng, as Alexander‡ or Cæsar.§ I am far from applauding such displays of absurd ambition ; but they are lessons, in the knowledge of mankind. Let not, then, young men, of talents superior to their condition, hastily consign themselves to an oblivious retreat, under the notion of practising a virtue, which may eventually

*Diogenes was a celebrated philosopher, who was born in Sinope, the capital of Pontus, in Asia Minor. He was banished from his native place, for coining false money. He then went to Athens, and became one of the sect called Cynics, who were famous for their contempt of riches, the negligence of their dress, and the length of their beards. He used to walk about the streets of Athens, with a tub upon his head. This tub served him as a house, and a place of repose. He died about 324, B. C. in the ninety-sixth year of his age.

† Simeon, a Syrian monk, who lived in the fifth century, invented a singular method of self-torture, about A. D. 423. He is said to have lived, for nine years, on the top of a column, or pillar, and afterwards changed his pillar for a higher one, and at length for one of sixty feet in height, and only three feet in diameter, at top. When he slept, he is said to have leaned against a sort of balustrade. The whole time, which he passed on the top of pillars, was about thirty-seven years, though during this period he descended several times. He submitted to this insane method of self-torture, by way of penance, and his example was imitated by many persons in Syria and Palestine, even so late as the twelfth century. These maniacs were called Stylites, from a Greek word, meaning a column ; and Simeon was canonized, or made a saint, after his death, by the Roman Catholic Church.

‡ Alexander,—see note on page 111.

§ Cæsar,—see notes on pages 59, and 212.

be a source of self-reproach.   If this be done, as I believe it sometimes is, with the secret hope of gaining reputation with the world, for an effort of philosophical self-denial, it may be depended upon, that such an inconsistency will fail of its purpose. The world is ready enough to forget the man who deserts it, and a wish for oblivion is soon literally gratified.   Johnson* has some excellent remarks on this topic, in his Life of Cowley,† which should be read by all, who entertain vague notions of the blessings of retirement and solitude, while they really pant after fame.

There is a class of losses, which, though they do not admit of restoration in kind, yet allow of *substitutions*, which may greatly alleviate the misfortune.   I have elsewhere enlarged considerably on the topic of substitution, as the most effectual remedy applicable to the case of consolation under the loss of friends by death.   In all others, of a similar class, the same relief should be sought after; and the pursuit of it requires the union of the spirit of resignation with that of resistance,— the first, to prepare the way for the second.   I have lost, probably for ever, that health, which fitted me for active services and enjoyments, and with it, many sources of happiness and utility. Shall I abandon myself to unavailing sorrow, and drag out a lifeless existence, in the inaction of despair ?   No.   My head and hands are still free ;

* *Dr. Samuel Johnson*, author of the Dictionary that is called by his name.

† A celebrated English poet, who was born A. D. 1618.

I can write, read, and converse. To these, then, I must look, for my future amusements and occupations, and I may yet make a good *salvage** for the remains of life. Cicero,† when deprived of his political existence, by the overthrow of the Roman constitution, thus writes to a friend : " Shall I vex and torment myself ? To what purpose ? You may live, you say, to letters. Do you think I employ myself in any thing else ? I could not live, at all, unless I lived to letters." In reality, this life of his has gained him more posthumous fame than all the busy scenes of his public life.

Many are the cases, in which substitution may successfully be applied, provided the mind be first brought to a proper temper. The loss of power and place may be compensated, by the rational use of leisure, and many have found it a most abundant compensation. Even the loss of liberty may be alleviated, by such a close occupation of the mind, in study, as will scarcely allow time for perceiving the want of it. Raleigh‡ wrote his

---

* *Salvage* is a reward, or recompense allowed by law, for saving a ship or goods, from loss at sea.

† See note on page 213.

‡ *Sir Walter Raleigh* was a distinguished warrior, statesman, and writer, who was born in Devonshire, England, A.D. 1552. He was in great favor with Queen Elizabeth, and, in 1584, proposed an expedition for the discovery and settlement of those parts of North America, not already visited by Christians. One of these expeditions terminated in the settlement of Virginia. He made several voyages, and traded with the Indians of different places ; and at last incurred the displeasure of King James, and was imprisoned for twelve years, du-

History of the World in prison, and probably was a happier man, during the composition of it, than while pursuing his golden speculations, among the poor Indians.   The admirable Grotius* so immersed himself in a variety of studies, during his confinement at the castle of Louvestein, that he lost all sense of the tediousness of his situation ; and other great scholars have rather regarded imprisonment as a favorable opportunity for completing some literary design, which the business of the world had impeded, than as a state of .suffering.   I can conceive of few greater misfortunes than the loss of sight ; yet we find it is often borne with cheerfulness, by indulging a social disposition, or cultivating a taste for music.   In all these instances, the substitute may at first appear very inadequate ; but it will grow more and more efficacious, the longer it is applied.   Let but the mind become interested in a pursuit, and it is surprising, what seemingly light and trivial objects will stand in the stead of those, which, in com-

ring which time he wrote his History of the World.   He was afterwards beheaded, by order of the King, October 29, 1618, in the sixty-fourth year of his age.

* *Hugo Grotius*, a celebrated scholar and statesman, was born April 10, 1583, at Delft, in Holland.   He was well educated, and wrote several works, particularly a Commentary on the New Testament, a work on the Truth of the Christian Religion, and a great work on Natural and National Law, in War and Peace.   He sustained several offices, and, owing to a controversy in which he was engaged, he was condemned to be imprisoned, for life, in the castle of Louvestein, but escaped.   He was afterwards ambassador from Sweden to France, for ten years.   He died August, 28, 1645.

mon estimation, infinitely exceed them in importance.

There are evils, however, which admit neither of removal nor of redress, by substitution ; and under the pressure of these, it is, that the virtue of quiet resignation is peculiarly indicated. Of this kind, is acute and incurable bodily pain, which absorbs the whole man, and puts to flight all thought but of itself. The only alleviation, of which it is capable, is to endure it with firmness and self-possession. This has a doubly good effect : it prevents those intemperate struggles, which aggravate the pain ; and it soothes the soul with a consciousness of its own strength. Though, as I have said, pain, in its extremity, occupies the whole attention of the sufferer, yet, during those remissions, which always, in some degree, attend it, other sensations steal in, which, if of an agreeable kind, have some effect in softening the violence of the entire paroxysm. It has always been observed, that pain is best borne, in the presence of spectators, the applause bestowed on fortitude operating as a sort of charm against it. Indeed, as even the pain called corporeal is felt through the medium of the mind, it is possible to conceive of mental emotions so strong, as to abolish all sense of pain ; but these cannot be applied, as ordinary remedies. Enthusiasm will, on some great emergencies, bear up the soul against all bodily torments ; but the enthusiastic temper is necessarily an unequal one, and therefore ill adapted to contend with a perpetually recurring evil, which rouses no particular passion or principle to resist it, but wears down the spirits, by incessant suffering. Hence, even in religious and political persecutions, enthusiasm is very apt to give way, under continued severities, while calm and equal courage endures to the last.

The infirmities of age, especially when accompanied with narrow circumstances, which no exertions, at that period, can improve, constitute an evil, or rather a combination of evils, only to be encountered by patient resignation ; and truly admirable is that composure of mind, which, as we often see, causes such a lot to be undergone with serenity, and even with cheerfulness. I do not add to the amount of the miseries of this condition, the fear of death, since death is their natural termination, and must be regarded, by a mind unimpressed with false terrors, as " a consummation devoutly to be wished for." That the dread of death, in such circumstances, is merely an artificial sentiment, I am fully convinced, from observation among that class of people whose feelings are least disturbed by fictitious notions, the product of leisure brooding over mysterious systems. These uniformly

Count death kind Nature's signal of retreat,

even independently of their aspirations after " a happier seat," though such a hope must undoubtedly contribute to gild the parting scene. Most beautifully has Goldsmith* said, of the path to the tomb, that

" Resignation gently slopes the way."

* *Oliver Goldsmith*, an eminent poet and miscellaneous

For this principle, the most solid foundation, certainly, is the religious conviction, that every thing is ordained for the greatest good, not only of the whole, but *of every individual.* This is a persuasion, which, if firmly entertained, one would suppose adequate to put an end to all murmuring and impatience, on account of evils merely temporary and remedial ; did not a thousand instances prove how feebly distant objects, seen only by the eye of the mind, act upon us, in comparison with those which are present, and obvious to sense. Moreover, I will not undertake to say, from what system the conviction abovementioned can be clearly deduced. But resignation is likewise a *habit,* induced by the constant practice of meeting every calamity with an unruffled, unperturbed mind. This may be formed by early discipline, in which every slight occurrence is employed as an essay or lesson ; and, in fact, they often prove as hard trials, in proportion to the acquired power of endurance, as the most serious evils, in afterlife. It is, therefore, of importance, to accustom one's-self to bear trivial losses and disappointments, without complaint ; for, by suppressing the external signs of emotion, the feeling itself comes, in time, to be brought under control. Nothing, relative to moral discipline, is indifferent ; all operates to confirm either good or bad habits.

writer, was born at Pallas, in Ireland, in 1731. Many of his works have been much celebrated and admired. He died in April, 1774

For you, my young reader, I wish, in the first place, that you may undergo as few trials from adverse fortune, as the human lot will permit : in the second place, I wish you may have spirit to resist and resignation to endure, in proportion to the demand that may be made upon you, for the exertion of either of these qualities.

THE END.

MESSRS. HARPER & BROTHERS have the pleasure of announcing that they have just issued a complete Classified and Descriptive Catalogue of their Publications, comprising a very extensive range of Literature, in its several departments of History, Biography, Philosophy, Travel, Science and Art, the Classics, and Fiction; also, many splendidly Embellished Productions. A rigid critical taste has governed the selection of these works, so as to include not only a large proportion of the most esteemed Literary Productions of our times, but supplying also, in the majority of instances, the best existing authorities on given subjects. This new Catalogue, having been constructed with a view to the especial use of persons desirous of forming or enriching their Literary Collections, as well as principals of District Schools and Seminaries of Learning, who may not possess any reliable means of forming a true estimate of any production, commends itself to all such by its novel feature of including bibliographical, explanatory, and critical notices. For want of such aid, a large portion of the reading community remain ignorant of the vast wealth of our accumulated literary stores, an acquaintance with which must ever be regarded as an essential element, both in the progress of social advancement and in individual refinement and happiness. It may be as well to add, that the valuable collection described in this Catalogue, consisting of about *eighteen hundred volumes*, combines the two-fold advantages of great economy in price with neatness —often great elegance of typographical execution, in many instances the rates of publication being scarcely one-fifth of those of similar issues in Europe.

*** Copies of this Catalogue may be obtained, free of expense, by application to the Publishers personally, or by letter, post-paid.

All orders accompanied with a remittance promptly executed.

82 Cliff-street, Sept., 1846.

3

WM

Check Out More Titles From HardPress Classics Series In this collection we are offering thousands of classic and hard to find books. This series spans a vast array of subjects – so you are bound to find something of interest to enjoy reading and learning about.

Subjects:
Architecture
Art
Biography & Autobiography
Body, Mind &Spirit
Children & Young Adult
Dramas
Education
Fiction
History
Language Arts & Disciplines
Law
Literary Collections
Music
Poetry
Psychology
Science
…and many more.

Visit us at www.hardpress.net

Im The Story
personalised classic books

JANE
IN
WONDERLAND

LEWIS
CARROLL

"Beautiful gift.. lovely finish.
My Niece loves it, so precious!"

Helen R Brumfieldon

⭐⭐⭐⭐⭐

UNIQUE
GIFT

FOR KIDS, PARTNERS
AND FRIENDS

Timeless books such as:

Kids

Alice in Wonderland   •   The Jungle Book   •   The Wonderful Wizard of Oz
Peter and Wendy   •   Robin Hood   •   The Prince and The Pauper
The Railway Children   •   Treasure Island   •   A Christmas Carol

Adults

Romeo and Juliet   •   Dracula

Highly Customizable

Change Book Title

Replace Characters names with yours

Upload Photo into inside page!

Add Inscriptions

Visit
Im The Story .com
and order yours today!

CPSIA information can be obtained
at www.ICGtesting.com
Printed in the USA
BVHW080121120819
555624BV00027B/4804/P